"Author Jeffrey John [barcode] _Glory_ that we are al̲ ̲ ̲ ̲ ̲ ̲ ̲ ̲ ̲ ̲ ̲ ̲ . ̲ ̲ ̲ ̲ ̲ ̲ ̲ ̲ ̲ . He is right. Every person who has ever lived is on a journey to find something of meaning and value in life. What are you pursuing—happiness, freedom, companionship, truth? The key to this search, as you will read in this book, is much more than 'what' you are looking for. Actually, the 'Who' of your search is all important. If you are honestly searching for the meaning and value of life as it is truly to be lived, read this volume from cover to cover. It will point you to finding glory in knowing Jesus Christ, the Son of God, who will give you purpose for your life now and hope for eternal life to come."

—Lance Quinn, senior pastor, Bethany Church, Thousand Oaks, California

"Jeffrey Johnson has provided a marvelously helpful little book that focuses on the real heart issues of life. This is an excellent book to give to both unbelievers and believers. As I read, I easily saw how this book could be used in evangelism as well as in basic counseling situations. It is well written, straightforward, pastorally wise, and full of Scripture. This book is a wonderfully useful tool in helping us get to the issues that drive our hearts and to see the all-satisfying Christ as the ultimate goal of all our pursuits. May the Lord use it to bring many to Himself and strengthen many of His children in a closer walk with Him."

—Brian Borgman, author of _Feelings and Faith_

"*The Pursuit of Glory* is must reading for every Christian. In it Jeffrey Johnson conveys major aspects of Christian living as they relate to glory. His topic is unusual, as it is often thought that only God has glory. Read with faith and know you too may pursue glory— for God is glory!"

—Jay Adams, author of *Competent to Counsel*

"What does your heart yearn for? What do the hearts of those you work with, live with, and serve yearn for? Jeff Johnson's *Pursuit of Glory* shines a spotlight on common desires that bubble up in all of us and often spill over, making a mess in our lives and in the lives of those we care about. He shows how the pursuit of glory, happiness, purpose, freedom, companionship, truth, peace, holiness, and life are created in us but can be satisfied only in Christ. Johnson illustrates our flawed ambitions to satisfy each of these desires from his rich background of life and ministry experiences. He presents these so that any of us can become more keenly aware of our own hearts. But I see richness here too for caring brothers and sisters who want to help others realign their hearts and lives with God's freeing grace after suffering from the world's, the flesh's, or the devil's seductive prescriptions."

—Rick Horne, author of *Get Offa My Case, Godly Parenting of an Angry Teen*, and *Get Outta My Face! How to Reach Angry, Unmotivated Teens with Biblical Counsel*

the pursuit of
Glory

the pursuit of
Glory

Finding Satisfaction in Christ Alone

Jeffrey D. Johnson

Reformation Heritage Books
Grand Rapids, Michigan

The Pursuit of Glory
© 2018 by Jeffrey D. Johnson

Reformation Heritage Books
2965 Leonard St. NE
Grand Rapids, MI 49525
616-977-0889
orders@heritagebooks.org
www.heritagebooks.org

Printed in the United States of America
18 19 20 21 22 23/10 9 8 7 6 5 4 3 2 1

Library of Congress Cataloging-in-Publication Data

Names: Johnson, Jeffrey D. (Pastor), author.
Title: The pursuit of glory : finding satisfaction in Christ alone / Jeffrey D. Johnson.
Description: Grand Rapids, Michigan : Reformation Heritage Books, 2018.
Identifiers: LCCN 2018005499 (print) | LCCN 2018008229 (ebook) | ISBN 9781601785992 (epub) | ISBN 9781601785985 (pbk. : alk. paper)
Subjects: LCSH: Glory of God—Christianity. | Satisfaction—Religious aspects—Christianity. | Pride and vanity—Religious aspects—Christianity.
Classification: LCC BT180.G6 (ebook) | LCC BT180.G6 J64 2018 (print) | DDC 234—dc23
LC record available at https://lccn.loc.gov/2018005499

For additional Reformed literature, request a free book list from Reformation Heritage Books at the above regular or e-mail address.

Dedicated to my loving wife,

Letha

Contents

Foreword

This book gives an expanded exposition of the Augustinian summary of human purpose, "You have made us for yourself, O God, and our hearts are restless until they find their rest in You." Jeff Johnson, the author, wants the reader to experience satisfaction in this universal quest and moves us toward the goal in three ways. The book title draws us to one set of important ideas. The list of chapter titles draws us to a second set. The style of argument makes us consider another important aspect of engaging this ultimately important subject.

The title may be considered as a twofold concern. First, we may view the pursuit of glory from a heavenly, or transcendent, perspective; second, it may be considered from an earthly, or immanent, perspective. From the transcendent side, a person's pursuit of glory (if it is a real pursuit of glory) will lead him or her to desire the forever-satisfying experience of seeing and living in the presence of God in all His glorious perfection. Those who truly desire this "transport of delight" finally will see Him as He is. Anne Cousins, a nineteenth-century writer, composed a song about what prompts the desire to be in heaven. Here are two of the verses:

O Christ, He is the fountain,
The deep, sweet well of love!
The streams on earth I've tasted
More deep I'll drink above:
There to an ocean fullness
His mercy doth expand,
And glory, glory dwelleth
In Immanuel's land.

The King there in His beauty,
Without a veil is seen:
It were a well-spent journey,
Though seven deaths lay between:
The Lamb with His fair army,
Doth on Mount Zion stand,
And glory—glory dwelleth
In Immanuel's land.

From the immanent side, the pursuit of glory will lead the seeker to find his or her sense of permanent well-being in having the character of God imprinted in his or her affections and actions. This is a book about those two ways of seeing glory and how God, in His grace, does indeed bring sinners into His "house of wine" again, as Anne Cousins expressed it:

O I am my Beloved's
And my Beloved's mine!
He brings a poor vile sinner
Into His house of wine.
I stand upon His merit—
I know no other stand,
Not e'en where glory dwelleth
In Immanuel's land.

The author gives a second major prompting to find rest for our restlessness in the hopes that form the titles of each chapter. Jeff gives a clear description of how each of these hopes resides within everyone. Every one of these is deeply embedded in the soul because the form (now really only a form, an empty shell) of these deeply and richly satisfying states of being is inextricably set as fundamental to human nature. These are the shapes of the divine image in humanity. They have been emptied of their content, but the shape is there, and that is the reason "our hearts are restless until they find their rest" in our Creator.

Glory, happiness, purpose, freedom, companionship, truth, peace, holiness, life—every person strives to find these in something that is a substitute for the real thing. The author, reflecting on Scripture as his authority and looking at examples in the lives of friends and persons he has counseled, sets the table in a compelling style. In a manner similar to the biblical book of Ecclesiastes, he demonstrates that all our attempts to substitute the values and things of this present age for that which is genuine without exception fail. The truth in each of these quests of soul resides in God alone. Attempts to find them in the creation instead of the Creator are sheer vanity—endlessly frustrating, severely disappointing, and horribly aggravating vanity.

The author's intention is not to condemn the quest for glory and all the fulfilling things that compose its reality. No, the pursuit is good and right. It is what we were made for. His intention, bolstered by his personal quest and his commitment to the revealed truth of Scripture, is to show how all these elements of the divine image are restored through the redemptive, reconciling work of Christ. He expands this by the way he weaves his argument.

The third inviting feature of this book has to do with its style of argument. It is composed of both propositions of truth and acute observations about the author's personal journey. Like Augustine in his spiritual testimony *Confessions*, Jeff Johnson has shared some deep conflicts of his own life in which he came up short of finding the thing he looked for. In one event, he was driven to the brink of suicide. By God's powerful, life-changing intervention in his life, however, that which he had despaired of finding in this life became his through the grace of Christ. His honest, transparent, plain-spoken, earnest accounts of how true glory, happiness, purpose, and the other elements of this pursuit flooded his own life are interwoven with the biblical truth supporting each element of his quest. This comes as an invitation to each of us to find it in the same way.

He is not proposing some secret, mystical incantation or detachment from reality but points to the plainly revealed, clearly proposed gospel of the birth, life, crucifixion, resurrection, and ascension of Jesus Christ. He is the one in whom all the fullness of the Godhead dwells in bodily form. Jesus is indeed the image of the invisible God, the express image of His character; He is the brightness of the Father's glory. If we seek glory and all its accompanying values, we will find them only in Christ. That is the driving purpose and clear message of this book. "Take and read."

Tom J. Nettles
Louisville, Kentucky

1

the pursuit of Glory

You and I are looking for something. Though we may not know exactly what it is, we continue to search for it. No matter how hard we try, we cannot stop our pursuit of it. As if we are looking for a lost wallet, we cannot rest until we find what is missing. We look here and then there without finding, and yet we continue to search.

We pursue it with all our heart for it consumes us. We are restless! Our drive to find it determines every decision we make. Even my desire to write and your desire to read this book were motivated by our common pursuit. We want it badly, but so does everyone. Whether or not we love God, the pursuit is in us all. It is part of the human condition. We were made by God to pursue it, and pursue it we will.

What is it, you may be wondering? What is it, you ask, that we cannot stop pursuing? It is glory. We are all looking for glory—*unadulterated glory*!

Not Earthly Glory

I do not mean fame, if that is what you are thinking. It is true that we are often deceived into looking for glory in becoming famous. Notoriety, however, has never brought any lasting satisfaction. Famous people are miserable too. They, along with each of us, have holes in their hearts that cannot be filled by mass numbers of Twitter followers.

This hole inside our hearts, that empty spot that longs to be filled, seeks for something far greater than being a celebrity. Deep down, we long for true glory. We long for the highest glory—the glory of glories—a glory that cannot be surpassed by earthly accolades—an unadulterated glory.

Being made in the image of God, we can never be satisfied with a counterfeit glory that is manufactured from the things of this world. Even the atheist Bertrand Russell understood that people can never be satisfied with the glory of this world: "Man differs from other animals in one very important respect, and that is that he has some desires which are, so to speak, infinite, which can never be fully gratified, and which would keep him restless even in Paradise."[1]

The only glory that can satisfy our deepest longings is not obtained at our favorite department store or at the Audi dealership. This glory is not found in throwing the game-winning pass in the Super Bowl or being elected president of the United States. Health, wealth, and power are all alluring, but deep down we all know that our hearts aspire for something that transcends these things. The glory we seek does not fade away. It is not empty or vain. Rather, true glory consists of something eternal—something weightier than things that perish.

Consider that the Hebrew word for glory, *kabowd*, means heaviness. Though this may seem like a strange way of

---

1. Bertrand Russell, as quoted in *Nobel Writers on Writing*, ed. Ottar G. Draugsvold (Jefferson, NC: McFarland, 2000), 61.

defining glory, we must remember that the value of ancient coins was determined by their weight—their heaviness. Today, a nickel is heavier than a dime, yet this was not the case when coins were made from precious metals. When you are trading with coins forged from bronze, silver, and gold, then the larger and heavier the coin is, the better. The greater the weight, the greater the value. Thus, the glory and value of something is in its weight, or substance.

The biblical contrast to glory is vanity. In Hebrew, *vanity* speaks of something having little to no substance. It speaks of that which is light, empty, or worthless. We may grasp the wind, but even if we were able to lay hold of it, what do we have? Nothing. There is no value in having a fistful of air.

Not Temporary Glory

To understand the difference between glory and vanity, we must discern the distinction between temporal and eternal realities. Because the praise of people and the glory of this world are passing away, they are superficial. They are vanity. Though on the surface they feel and look impressive, underneath the shine lies a hidden and expanding layer of corrosion.

For the person who has mere seconds to live, what does it really matter if he or she has a handful of weeds or a handful of rubies? Nothing really matters if all we have are things we cannot keep. As the psalmist observes, our "plans perish" with us at death (Ps. 146:4). Even if we could gain the whole world before dying, what value would it be to us if we lost our souls afterward (Mark 8:36)?

The glory of this world is like a dissipating vapor. And we all, deep down in our consciences, know it. We know that earthly beauty and praise is short-lived. At best, the most attractive things in this world are like beautiful flowers that have already begun to wilt. The diminishing glory of this world is like the grimy canals and the years of decay that have settled on Venice, Italy. It is just a matter of time before its splendor will disappear altogether.

Searching after the glory of this world is like grasping after the wind. The instant you think you have it, it slips away from you like the smell of a new car that begins to fade the moment the car is driven off the lot. Earthly triumphs are soon forgotten. Trophies that once stood proudly on the mantle are now boxed away in the attic. Even the memories of your "glory days"—when you were the star basketball player or you graduated magna cum laude—are starting to grow dim. It will not be long before almost everything, if not everything, about your life will be forgotten.

Death overtakes us all. The stench of it has penetrated the fabric of life. The brevity of life is ever present in our minds; it taints our most joyful experiences. No matter what enjoyment you and I find in the here and now, we subconsciously know that the grim reaper is lurking for us in the shadows.

The world and all its desires are passing away (1 John 2:17). All earthly glory is fleeting—"riches are not forever" (Prov. 27:24). Therefore, as the Preacher says, the glory of this world is vanity. The best this world has to offer is empty and meaningless. "All *is* vanity" (Eccl. 1:2, emphasis added).

Not Superficial Glory

Nothing in this life is permanent. Thus, we pursue an eternal glory. I do not mean that we long to live forever in our current state. Mere existence is hell if it is all we have to look forward to. We do not long merely to stay alive; rather, we long to obtain something that is more important than what this world offers. Again, we are searching for an unadulterated glory.

Whatever this glory is, it is something that is far weightier, far more valuable, far more precious, and far more lasting than that which can be mined out of this world. The glory that we need is an eternal glory. It is an infinite, unchanging, and immeasurable glory. This is the only thing that will fully and eternally satisfy us.

This glory is found only in God. Because there is no enduring value in perishable things, we cannot help but desire an "eternal weight of glory" (2 Cor. 4:17). This is why we all, whether we acknowledge it or not, are in pursuit of the glory of God. It is the only thing that truly matters in life because God alone is eternal, infinite, and immutable. Only God is of infinite value. Everything else is vain, empty, and worthless in comparison. God's glory is the sum of all that God is. It is the radiance, majesty, beauty, and splendor that shine forth from His unchangeable and eternal essence.

Because glory is the value of the intrinsic worth of the essence of God, God's glory requires an observer. This does not mean that God's glory requires us to appreciate Him. His glory would not be eternal if it depended on anything outside Him. God's glory is eternal because God the Father, God the Son, and God the Holy Spirit have always appreciated and ascribed glory to one another. Because the Father knows the true value of the Son and the Spirit, He glorifies the Son and the Spirit. And the Son and the Spirit likewise know the true value of the Father, and they glorify the Father accordingly. This is the glory that they ascribed to each other from the beginning (John 17:5). They are completely and forever satisfied in the infinite glory they share with each other.

This is perfect glory. Because each person of the Trinity interpenetrates the other two, they know each other perfectly. Because of this perfect knowledge of each other, they have perfect, full appreciation of and love for each other. The Father is satisfied in the love of the Son and the Spirit, as the Son is satisfied in the love of the Father and the Spirit, and as the Spirit is satisfied in the love of the Father and the Son. Nothing lacking, nothing missing, nothing wanting. Full and complete satisfaction. This is the glory of God. And this is the only glory that can satisfy us. We are miserable not because we aspire after glory but because we aspire after glory in all the wrong things. That is, we don't aim high enough.

Again, all of us, whether we like it or not, are pursuing glory with all our hearts. It is not a matter of whether we look for glory; it is a matter of whether we look for glory in the only place glory can truly be found—in God. Therefore, the ultimate question is this: Do you long to enjoy the glory of God, or are you chasing the vainglory of this fallen world? In other words, what is your glory?

How you answer this question will determine everything. As this book seeks to explain, we long for happiness, purpose, freedom, companionship, truth, peace, holiness, and life. These longings are innate within us because we are made in the image of God. And, as we shall see, it is only when we find God that we find the glory we so desperately seek and need.

God has placed this longing—and what a longing it is—in our hearts (Acts 17:26–28). Being made in the likeness of God, we cannot be satisfied with anything less than the glory of God. As Augustine said so many years ago: "For Thou hast made us for Thyself and our hearts are restless, until they can find rest in Thee."[2]

ꙮ QUESTIONS FOR REFLECTION

1. What are the key differences between earthly and heavenly glory?

2. Why is the concept of weightiness used to describe the word *glory*?

3. Why does the Bible contrast the word *glory* with the word *vanity*?

4. How should contemplating death influence the way we view this world?

5. Where should we look to find glory?

---

2. Augustine, *Confessions*, trans. F. J. Sheed, ed. Michael P. Foley (London: Hackett, 2006), 3.

the pursuit of Happiness

The world is depressed. This is not hyperbole. Antidepressant medication is big business. According to Harvard Medical School and the National Center for Health Statistics, one out of every ten Americans is prescribed these "happy pills."[1] But this should not surprise us. Many people who are not trying to drown out their discontentment with medication seek escape through the constant distraction of noise, hedonistic pleasures, and entertainment. They are always buying, always shopping, always looking, always in pursuit—but never truly happy.

By *happiness* I do not mean enjoying physical pleasure. Sex, drugs, and rock 'n' roll offer a moment of sensual gratification, but I have never counseled a single addict who confessed to being happy. Enjoying a moment of pleasure, no matter how many times it is repeated, is not the same thing as happiness.

True happiness is enduring gratification and joy that is "inexpressible and full of glory" (1 Peter 1:8). It is the

---

1. Peter Wehrwein, "Astounding Increase in Antidepressant Use by Americans," *Harvard Health Blog*, Harvard Health Publishing, October 20, 2011, http://www.health.harvard.edu/blog/astounding-increase-in-antidepressant-use-by-americans-201110203624.

transcended glory of feeling satisfied, the perpetual contentment that is rooted in the soul. This type of happiness brings deep and lasting contentment. And this type of contentment is what every person longs to obtain. Blaise Pascal was right when he said, "All men seek happiness."[2] We cannot help but long for happiness. You and I cannot stop looking for it—even if we wanted to. No one can honestly say, "I do not want to be happy." Even if you think such a thought, it is only because you are tired of looking for it.

Every decision we make is motivated by our pursuit of happiness. Even giving up on happiness and committing suicide is a way of trying to find happiness through the back door. This was true for me. After feeling depressed for months, I sought to end my own life. At the end of my second year in college, I remember cleaning my room and loading my Makarov 9mm pistol. After weeks of suicidal ideation, I was ready for it all to end.

The misery, the hurt, and the darkness were all too much to bear. After I had all my affairs in order, with the loaded gun in hand, I felt that I needed to tie up one more loose end—telling my parents goodbye. I hoped that my dad and mom would not be too disappointed with my decision, but during my conversation with my dad, he gave me a small ray of hope, enough light to cause me to push the gun across the carpet and get on my knees and pray to God. That was twenty years ago, and as I look back, I realize that I did not want to die—I just did not want to live. My desire to kill myself was only a desire to kill the pain. As delusional as it may sound,

---

2. Blaise Pascal, *Pensées*, trans. A. J. Krailsheimer (London: Penguin, 1995), 45.

my desire to die was motivated by my unquenchable desire to be happy.

Since then I have counseled multiple suicidal people. Most people who follow through with it do so without any sign or warning. One day I would counsel a person, and the next day I would learn from a police official that the person had died and the cause of death was self-inflicted. This has happened to me twice. One of the hardest funerals I have ever preached was for a young man who overdosed with a suicide note in his hands.

The point is, we cannot make any decision that is *not* motivated by our desire to be happy. Even doing things we do not enjoy, like getting up and going to work, is motivated by our pursuit of happiness. Getting paid and paying our bills seem to be happier options than losing our jobs. Either immediate happiness or future happiness is behind everything we do.

Our problem is not that we want to be happy—this is God given. Rather, our problem lies in our unwillingness to seek happiness in God. We were made to be happy because we were made to enjoy and glorify God. But when we refuse to glorify God it is because we are deceived in thinking that happiness is found in things that cannot bring any true satisfaction.

Not Found in Us
First, it is easy to think happiness is found in loving ourselves. That is, we look for happiness in the things we love, and one of the easiest things for us to love is ourselves. Who does not love their own self? Moreover, the things we love

are the things we enjoy and treasure. And because we naturally treasure ourselves, we are tempted to look for happiness from within.

The more we look to find happiness in self-love, however, the lonelier and more miserable we become. We may not like to admit it, but we are not good enough even for ourselves. We are longing for unadulterated glory, and we—even in our best state—fall short of this glory. We are not sufficient to satisfy the deep longing of our hearts.

Though we may have a hard time acknowledging it, we cannot help but be disappointed in ourselves. This is because God did not design us to be self-sufficient or create us with happiness built in. We are deficient by our nature. Only God is sufficiently happy within Himself. Alone, the triune God is complete and eternally happy; He needs nothing. He alone is good enough for Himself.

In contrast, we were not designed to be alone. As God observed after placing Adam in the garden, "It is not good that man should be alone" (Gen. 2:18). We were not designed to be independent and self-sufficient. We are dependent and needy people, and we know it. By nature we are created with a hole in our heart that only the glory of God can fill. If we already possessed happiness, then we would not be in search of it. The fact that we enter the world crying tells us that we are not born with happiness preinstalled. Because we are dependent beings, we need to find happiness outside ourselves.

Well-intended therapists, along with our misguided friends, may encourage us to find happiness from within. They may tell us that we need to take more time to pamper ourselves. They may even tell us that we need to learn to love ourselves—as if a lack of self-love was ever the problem. But they have no idea what they are saying.

Tell the man who is abandoned on a small deserted island to find happiness from within himself. Tell the person in isolation, with nothing to look forward to, that all he needs is his own thoughts to be happy. Tell the lonely person that all she needs to be happy is to spend quality time with herself. Such advice is foolish because isolation will drive anyone mad. Isolation is a form of punishment. It is a characteristic of hell itself. Telling us to spend more time thinking about ourselves is only encouraging us to become more self-absorbed, and this is part of the problem, not the answer.

Not Found in Materialism

The root problem is that we are born isolated from the only true source of lasting happiness—God. This spiritual isolation is the reason we are in search of happiness. Because we do not have God, we are in a search to fill that void. And because we, by nature, do not want God, we are drawn to look for happiness in something other than God, such as materialism. As Henry Scougal remarked, "The soul of man, in its pursuit of happiness, has a raging and inextinguishable thirst—an immaterial kind of fire—that is always grasping at one object or another."[3] And this is the second pitfall that we are prone to fall into—the temptation to seek happiness in worldly things.

---

3. Henry Scougal, *The Life of God in the Soul of Man* (Conway, Ark.: Free Grace Press, 2017), 90.

Being materialistic comes naturally to us all. From the day we enter the world, we begin crying for things. As a new parent, I learned quickly that I could not allow my oldest son to think he was entitled to a new toy every time we entered the superstore. Though his toy box was already overflowing with all kinds of crazy gadgets and noisemakers, it was not enough. "More, more, more!" was his cry. Sadly, the great majority of even teenagers and adults have yet to learn that toys and trucks never satisfy. Just how much stuff do we need before we no longer feel envious? How much is enough?

It is not that material things are evil in themselves. God created "all things" in this world for us "richly...to enjoy" (1 Tim. 6:17). God loves giving gifts as an expression of His love for us. Just like receiving a Valentine card from our spouse draws us closer to him or her, God's gifts are designed to draw our affections to Him.

The things that are visible, like the heavens and the sky, are meant to push our hearts and minds to treasure the invisible glory of God (Ps. 19:1). Yet in our selfishness, we have used the very things that were designed to point our affections toward God to draw our affections away from Him. We have turned God's gifts against Him by molding them into idols (Rom. 1:23). That is, we desire God's gifts without desiring God. We want the creation without the Creator.

Our depraved hearts spoil everything. Rather than seeking happiness in the infinite Giver, we foolishly seek happiness in the finite gifts. Rather than eating and drinking for the glory of God, we eat and drink for the glory of self. We have perverted those things God has created for our good, such as sex, food, and drink, by turning them into self-destructive vices. Rather than glorifying God, we "glory…in [our] shame" (Phil. 3:19).

No wonder we are so miserable. Like looking for water inside a rock, we foolishly continue to search for an infinite amount of happiness in perishable and physical things that are able to give us only a small amount of fleeting pleasure. We are deceived in thinking that feeding the lusts of our flesh will somehow satisfy the inherent longings of our souls.

Rather than offering enjoyment, these finite pleasures leave us disappointed. We often end up despising them for their inability to provide us with the lasting happiness and contentment we so desperately crave. What God has designed for our enjoyment, we have used to create a deeper sense of dissatisfaction.

The problem is not that we have physical cravings. The Lord Jesus had physical cravings—He grew hungry and thirsty. Cravings come from being deficient of something we need. As finite beings, God created us to need things, such as food and water.

The infinite "God cannot be tempted" (James 1:13) because He does not need anything (Acts 17:25). What could possibly entice the immutable God who lacks nothing? We, on the other hand, are not self-sufficient. We are tempted because we have needs. Even Christ, as He entered into the weaknesses of human flesh, was "tempted as we are" (Heb. 4:15). Yet having cravings and needs is not the cause of sin, for Christ was tempted without falling into sin.

The cause of sin stems from a heart that desires to satisfy a legitimate craving with an illegitimate experience. It is not sinful to desire clothes, food, drink, and sex. It is sinful when we make idols of these things. It is sinful when these desires move us to place our self-interests above the interests of others. It is sinful when we become discontent with the provisions God has given us. In short, it is sinful when we pervert that which is meant for our good.

In His goodness, God did not create us to have needs so that we would be miserable. Rather, He created us to have needs so that we could enjoy pleasurable moments with thankfulness to Him. God could have withheld taste buds so that eating would be drudgery. All food could have tasted like rice cakes if God was against pleasure. Procreation could have been boring. Thankfully, however, God made fulfilling our needs to be a means of pleasure. We should thank God that seeing, hearing, feeling, tasting, and smelling are enjoyable experiences.

God has provided us with legitimate and enjoyable satisfaction for all our legitimate cravings. God has promised to meet all our needs (Phil. 4:19). When God created Adam to desire a wife, He provided him with Eve to satisfy this need. Adam and Eve would require food, and God placed them in a garden to fulfill their hunger. They could eat the fruit from every tree but one. The whole garden was essentially theirs to richly enjoy.

Yet of all the trees in the garden, it was the forbidden one that Satan used to tempt them. It was not as if they were hungry or lacking food; they had everything they needed. Life was perfect. And in the midst of being well cared for by God, they were tempted to defy Him by taking the one thing that did not belong to them. Having everything, they became discontent.

Likewise, we fall into sin when we are not thankful and satisfied with the provisions that God has gracefully given us. God has given us more than we need, but we are tempted to want what we do not have. We are ungrateful. We find ourselves coveting our neighbor's car and overindulging ourselves with the things we do have. We become gluttons with little to no moderation. We corrupt the good things that God has given us to enjoy by turning them into self-serving idols. When we should be thankful, we have become dissatisfied. Oh, what a sinful heart we have!

All this happens when we take our affections off Christ. Without Christ, we cannot help but be discontent. Even if we could obtain the whole world, we still would not have enough to be satisfied. This is because the finite and perishable things of this world were not designed to fill the God-shaped hole in our hearts.

When we could quench our thirst by drinking living water from the well of Christ (John 4:14), we continue to drink polluted water from broken cisterns that leave us even thirstier (Jer. 2:13). In pursuing this world, we become foolish and irrational. Our minds become blinded by "the deceitfulness of riches" of this world (Mark 4:19). We were made to enjoy God but have traded His glory for worthless knick-knacks that can never satisfy (Isa. 55:2).

Not Found in Physical Pleasure

Being spiritually dead, we are more enamored with perishable things that can be seen and felt than by the imperishable things that cannot be discerned by our senses. Being spiritually blind to the glory of God, we exchange His glory for meaningless items that can be seen, felt, smelled, heard, and tasted. As Thomas Aquinas stated, "Man cannot live without joy; therefore when he is derived of true spiritual joys it is necessary that he become addicted to carnal pleasures."[4]

Though we are dead toward God, we are very much alive to this world. Our five senses connect our souls to physical things. This is not bad, but without spiritual awakening, our depraved hearts are drawn away from the invisible God by hedonistic pursuits that can bring pleasure only to the senses.

This happened when Adam and Eve took their eyes off God and placed them on the forbidden fruit. They saw that it looked "pleasant to the eyes" (Gen. 3:6), and they became covetous of things that did not rightfully belong to them. Adam and Eve fell into misery because they just *had* to taste and experience the one thing that was forbidden. Motivated by their quest for happiness, they became dejected and miserable for the first time. Their relationship with God was marred, and this separation from God brought dissatisfaction to them and to the whole human race. Since then, humanity has been miserable and unsuccessfully searching for the happiness that was lost long ago. People have been blinded to the glory of God by the superficial glory of this world.

Looking, tasting, feeling, smelling, and hearing are the cravings of the flesh, but these cravings can never quench the lust of our heart. "The eye is not satisfied with seeing, nor the ear filled with hearing" (Eccl. 1:8) because the sensual things of this world, in and of themselves, were not designed to satisfy the longings of the soul. Though they can bring a burst of pleasure to our bodies, they cannot bring us to God—the

---

4. Thomas Aquinas, *Summa Theologica,* in *Great Books of the Western World*, vols. 19–20, trans. Fathers of the English Dominican Province, rev. Daniel J. Sullivan (Chicago, Ill.: Encyclopedia Britannica, 1952), II-II, q. 35, art. 4, ad. 2.

source of inward and lasting happiness. Moreover, living for fleshly passions only increases the appetite for fleshly things. The more we seek satisfaction from the things of this world, the more we will become discontent with this world. We will never have enough (Prov. 27:20).

No matter how seemingly gratifying it is to look at pornography, afterward it only creates a deeper burning and discontentment within us. Like drinking saltwater, the pleasures of this world only make us thirstier. Throwing oil on a fire only enlarges the flames, and by feeding our lusts, we only increase our insatiable appetites.

But this is not the worst of it. The pleasure of sin lasts only for a few moments, but the miserable consequences can linger indefinitely. It is fun to swipe a credit card, but it isn't pleasant to pay the bill. On the surface, the rock 'n' roll lifestyle may seem exciting, but after the flashing lights are turned off and the fans go home, the addictions and the broken homes remain. The rusty hook is always hidden behind the shiny bait. We think we can enjoy the enticing lure without getting caught in the snare. We think we can enjoy the drugs without becoming addicted. But the moment of pleasure is soon replaced with permanent scarring. Truly, in the long run, "the way of the unfaithful is hard" (Prov. 13:15). No matter what we pursue, as long as we refuse Christ, we are exchanging lasting happiness for a few moments of pleasure.

Not Found in Selfishness

Living for pleasure is living for self. Our fleshly appetites can seek to satisfy only our flesh, which is why selfishness is manifested by the works of the flesh, such as greed, covetousness, and jealousy. This is also the reason we argue, fight, and war with each other (James 4:1). With thousands of Lego pieces in their toy box, why do children argue over a single piece? Why do thieves steal? Why do spouses commit adultery? Why do people hurt each other? It is because they want what they do not have. They are selfish, depraved, and blinded to the glory of God. They believe that feeding their passions is the way to happiness, but greed, covetousness, and jealousy are the evidences of their deep-felt misery.

Not Found Anywhere but in God

Not only does discontentment cause us to fight one another but it causes us to fight God. Without God's grace, we do not love Him. Though we are in need of God, we do not want Him. We are blind to the glory of God by the superficial glory of this world. Thus, we have no interest in pursuing God with all our hearts because we do not want to stop pursuing the things of this world. And this is the reason, according to Henry Scougal, that though "all men pursue happiness, most of the world continues miserable."[5]

To find happiness we must find it in God. According to Jonathan Edwards, God is the "only happiness with which our souls can be satisfied."[6] And C. S. Lewis said: "God cannot give us a happiness and peace apart from Himself,

---

[5]. Henry Scougal, "The Fourth Reflection," in *The Works of Henry Scougal* (Morgan, Pa.: Soli Deo Gloria, 2002), 261.

[6]. Jonathan Edwards, "The True Christian's Life a Journey towards Heaven," in *The Works of Jonathan Edwards, Volume 17, Sermons and Discourses, 1730–1733*, ed. Mark Valeri (New Haven, Conn.: Yale University Press, 1999), 437; *The Works of Jonathan Edwards Online*, edwards.yale.edu.

because it is not there. There is no such thing."[7] But to go to God, we must forsake everything else, even our own selves (Matt. 19:29). We must pursue God with all our heart, with all our mind, and with all our strength.

Yet this is the problem. Our selfishness will not allow us to let go of our silly idols. Though death is certain, we would rather have our ten minutes of pleasure than find eternal happiness in God. We would rather be miserable forever than to surrender the things we know we cannot keep. C. S. Lewis claimed: "It would seem that Our Lord finds our desires not too strong, but too weak. We are half-hearted creatures, fooling about with drink and sex and ambition when infinite joy is offered us, like an ignorant child who wants to go on making mud pies in a slum because he cannot imagine what is meant by the offer of a holiday at the sea. We are far too easily pleased."[8]

I have been told that raccoons, with their human-like hands, can be trapped by placing a shiny object in a wooden box with a tiny hole in it. This is because raccoons are curious. To catch them in such a contraption the hole needs to be large enough for them to wiggle their hand into but small enough that they cannot retract it after grasping the shining object inside. If they would just let go of the item, they could slide their hands back out and be free. But raccoons are not just curious, they are stubborn.

And so it is with us—we refuse to let go of the fool's gold in our hands, and thus we remain entrapped in the cage of

---

7. C. S. Lewis, *Mere Christianity* (New York: Touchstone, 1996), 54.
8. C. S. Lewis, *The Weight of Glory: And Other Addresses* (New York: HarperOne, 2001), 26.

our own misery. The rich young ruler wanted to follow Jesus, but he did not want to forsake his riches. And though he kept his wealth, he went away impoverished and sad (Mark 10:22). What is it that you are tempted to hold on to? Whatever it is, it is not worth it. Though you may think you cannot be happy without it, it is the very thing keeping you from happiness.

Every idol must be forsaken, for it is impossible to serve two masters. Christ said to love one is to hate the other (Matt. 6:24). That is, we cannot treasure Christ if we treasure this world. Christ went on to say, "If anyone desires to come after Me, let him deny himself, and take up his cross, and follow Me. For whoever desires to save his life will lose it, but whoever loses his life for My sake will find it" (Matt. 16:24–25). "The love of the world and the love of God," according to Henry Scougal, "are like the scales of a balance—as the one falls, the other rises."[9] We will not forsake our idols until we see their vanity. And as Charles Spurgeon said: "Nothing teaches us about the preciousness of the Creator as much as when we learn the emptiness of everything else."[10]

If we live for this world, then we will remain discontent with this world. If we live for things that are empty and cannot satisfy, it is impossible to be satisfied. Yet if our happiness is in the Lord, then we can truly enjoy the physical blessings that God has given us. People who have surrendered all to God can enjoy either a steak dinner or a hot dog because they are content with little or with much. Truly King Solomon was right when he said that the wicked remain wanting (Prov.

---

9. Scougal, *Life of God in the Soul of Man*, 90.
10. Charles Spurgeon, *Evening by Evening*, revised and updated by Alistair Begg (Wheaton, Ill.: Crossway, 2007), 339.

10:3), but the righteous have enough to satisfy their appetite (Prov. 13:25).

The only way to fully enjoy the things of this world is by having a heart that is happy to live without the things of this world. When a person's life is not tied to the things of this world, then the things of this world are no longer a curse, but a blessing. As Henry Scougal explained:

> Those who find pleasure in God will find pleasure in every situation. Temporal enjoyments become all the more pleasurable when we taste the divine goodness in them, and consider them as tokens of God's love.[11]

The apostle Paul, for instance, had every reason to be miserable. Even though he was in prison, not knowing if he was going to live or die, he was rejoicing (Phil. 1:18). This is because his joy was not rooted in himself or in the things of this world or in earthly pleasures, but in God. He had discovered that the secret to contentment was to live for the glory of God (Phil. 4:11–12).

And as it was with Paul, it is only when we can say, "For to me, to live is Christ," that we will be able to say, "and to die is gain" (Phil. 1:21). We can lose everything—even life itself—and still rejoice. When we have placed our treasure in heaven, then no earthly circumstance can rob us of our joy (Matt. 6:20). Neither health, nor sickness, nor riches, nor poverty, nor life, nor death can tarnish true happiness.

Are you happy? If not, turn everything over to Christ. If you are not a Christian, then you will never have the joy you are looking for as long as you refuse to look to the Lord Jesus.

---

11. Scougal, *Life of God in the Soul of Man*, 52.

And if you are a Christian, then your discontent comes by taking your eyes off Christ.

Regardless, we must crucify the flesh daily and surrender all our desires over to the lordship of Christ. We must relinquish our finances, our careers, our marriages, and even our lives to find that which can never be taken from us. We must think and pray as did Henry Scougal: "I am persuaded, O God, I am persuaded that I can never be happy till my carnal and corrupt affections be mortified, the pride and vanity of my spirit be subdued, and I come seriously to despise the world and think nothing of myself."[12]

Only those whose lives are fully surrendered to the Lord find a joy that is unspeakable and full of glory. As the Puritan William Gurnall warned: "O take heed of this squint eye to our profit, pleasure, honour; or anything beneath Christ and heaven; for they will take away your heart, as the prophet said of wine and women, that is, our love, and if our love be taken away, there will be little courage left for Christ."[13]

Conclusion

In the end, what is the answer to our quest for happiness? It is not found in laboring and toiling for that which can never satisfy (Isa. 55:2). Rather, we can have true satisfaction only when we search for Christ with all our heart (Jer. 29:13). Christ must be our treasure, our pursuit, and our all. And those who find Christ find that He is enough. Only God's unadulterated glory is sufficient to fill the hole in our hearts. We are designed to

---

12. Scougal, *Life of God in the Soul of Man*, 65.
13. William Gurnall, *The Christian in Complete Armour* (Edinburgh: Banner of Truth, 1995), 1:18.

pursue happiness, but happiness is found only in God. Happy is the man whose God is the Lord (Ps. 33:12).

⸖ QUESTIONS FOR REFLECTION

1. How would you define *happiness*?

2. Why is happiness not found within us?

3. Why is happiness not found in materialism?

4. Why is happiness not found in physical pleasures?

5. Why is happiness found only in God?

the pursuit of *Purpose*

Every new day looked like yesterday for her. Day after day and year after year, she did the same thing: following a restless night of sleep, she pulled herself out of bed, walked to her chair in the living room, turned on the TV, and waited to go to sleep that night, only to repeat the process the next day. For two years I visited her about once a month. Besides me and the pizza delivery guy, she had no one to come see her. She lived alone, had no friends, and she would have nothing to do with her family. Her life consisted of one thing—watching television. As you would imagine, she was depressed, bitter, and miserable. The problem behind her misery is that she knew she was wasting her life away. Watching TV can be entertaining, but it does not accomplish anything worthwhile. In fact, living for television was the thing that was robbing her of real purpose.

Would you be happy if this was all your life consisted of? But how is your life any different? A little less TV maybe, but what is it that makes your life any more worthwhile?

If this is not a sad enough case, I have another one for you. I was once asked to go visit a lady who was dying of emphysema. She had only days to live. As I visited with her a few days before she died, she did something astonishing right before my eyes. She lit a cigarette and drew the smoke into her lungs by using the trachea hole in her neck.

Knowing that smoking was killing her, I asked her why she did not stop. She gave me an honest but pitiful answer: "I do not have anything else to live for." You could hear the sadness in her voice and see the hopelessness in her eyes, for her purpose in life consisted of smoking cigarettes. The thing she lived for was the thing that killed her.

How sad, but this is true of most everyone. Maybe we do not live to smoke, but how is living for other temporal pleasures any different? On our deathbed, are we going to look back and be proud of all the movies we watched and the bags of cheese puffs we consumed? The apostle Paul writes, "For the kingdom of God is not eating and drinking"—nor is it watching television (Rom. 14:17).

Without purpose, life is meaningless. And because none of us can bear the thought of a meaningless life, we crave purpose. We want to know that our lives mean something. We are looking not just for meaning but to prove our value to ourselves and to others. We need to know that our lives count for something—something greater than watching TV and smoking cigarettes. We long to know that we are not wasting space. We want a life that matters. Whether we like it or not, the pursuit for meaning and purpose is in us all.

Looking for Meaning in What We Do

We cannot help but look for self-identity and purpose in the things we do. It is hard for us not to allow our jobs to define us. Who am I? The answer you or I may give, such as "I am a physics teacher," or "I am an artist," has a way of defining us. This is why many of us seek to find our identity and self-worth in the things we do. This is not altogether a bad thing, but no matter how noble our calling may be, no job or hobby can provide us any ultimate purpose. Ultimate purpose can be found only in God.

When we refuse to live for God, however, we cannot help but realize that there is nothing to live for at all. If God is dead, as the German philosopher Friedrich Nietzsche claimed, then we must conclude man's purpose is also dead. As did Solomon years before (Eccl. 1:12–18), the French Nobel Prize winner Albert Camus came to a conclusion about the vanity of life. In his philosophical essay *The Myth of Sisyphus*, Camus compared life to the ancient myth of Sisyphus, who was cursed to carry a heavy rock up a steep mountain that became steeper as he climbed. The closer he came to reaching his goal, the more difficult the process became until, finally, it was impossible. It was inevitable at a certain point in his journey that the boulder would fall off his back and roll all the way down to the base of the mountain. Turning around in despair, Sisyphus realized, as he marched down after his stone, that his lot in life was to repeat this grinding process over and over without end.

Hard work is manageable when there is a reason or motive to work, but when the work becomes pointless, then despair is all that remains. Life and all its meaningless labor amount to nothing. We live and hope for tomorrow, but tomorrow only brings us closer to death.

For instance, an activist group must have felt proud of themselves after they spent months nursing a wounded sea lion back to health. I remember seeing the video of the big day when the sea lion was being released into the ocean. The news cameras and spectators were all there to cheer on the beloved animal. Yet, within seconds of being set free, all the applause stopped and everything went quiet when the sea lion was quickly gulped up and eaten by a shark. What seemed to be the moment of liberation turned into the ultimate defeat.

But the wasted effort given to nursing the sea lion back to health is indicative of all our labor. We remodel houses, fix roads, and save lives only to know that our efforts buy only a little more time. Soon everything we do is going to be undone and forever forgotten.

Some people have given their lives to watching television and others to building their careers. But a successful life is not determined by accomplishing anything that is bound to perish in the end. Sooner or later every sea lion is sure to die. The point is, once we feel like the benefit of our labor is no longer worth the investment, we will cease to be motivated to work at all. But if life is pointless, as Camus observed, why even live?

Many people are tempted to give up and succumb to laziness. But laziness only compounds our sense of worthlessness. It is easy to be lazy. All we have to do is do nothing. More than a few times I have walked into the gym, only to say to myself, "I just do not feel like it today," and then went right back out to my car. It is fun to sit on the couch, eat popcorn, and watch a little TV. And who does not like to sleep in every now and then?

A few relaxing vacation days are helpful, but doing nothing day after day will cause us to feel worthless. Idleness is easy and fun for the moment, but it leaves us feeling empty afterward. Eating a box of donuts and lying around can be enjoyable, but we have nothing to show for it at the end of the day except for a few extra calories and a sense of regret (Prov. 6:9–11).

Laziness is like blowing our hard-earned money on needless stuff—it is fun for the moment, but afterward we have buyer's remorse and wish we would have used our money and time more wisely. It is one thing to oversleep and waste a few hundred dollars here and there, but what if we are wasting our entire lives away? How will we feel when God asks us how we invested the resources He gave us?

No wonder so many men feel miserable when they are in their midtwenties and still living with their parents and playing video games all day. The best feeling they have is when they conquer level 9 in record time. And it is no surprise that many women feel useless as they lie around the house eating Ben & Jerry's Chubby Hubby ice cream and watching daytime soap operas.

While snowboarding in Colorado, I met a young man who moved to Breckenridge so he could hit the slopes every day. I remember him bragging, "I want my life to be like your vacation." Though he thought I would be envious, I went away feeling sorry for him. Sure, he is going to have a killer time, but unless he changes his mind and gets a job, killing time will be all that he accomplishes with his life.

Rather than feeling the thrill of victory after practicing hard and outperforming their opponents, now athletes are rewarded a participation trophy and can avoid the agony of defeat. Everyone is entitled to win. Instead of allowing those who work hard to enjoy the fruitfulness of their labor, our culture wants to rob the rich and give it to those who refuse to work.

Rewarding laziness does no one any good. God says, "If anyone will not work, neither shall he eat" (2 Thess. 3:10). We are to labor with our hands (1 Thess. 4:11), for God did not create us to be lazy. From the beginning He created us to work, and to work hard (Gen. 2:15).

Adam and Eve were given responsibilities in the garden. Life was meant to be more than eating, drinking, and being merry. God gave people responsibilities to fulfill, and these responsibilities provided them with meaning and purpose—something worthwhile to accomplish.

Work is meant to bring us a sense of purpose. As much as I procrastinate, I really enjoy yard work. I take pride in doing a good job. I edge the sidewalk, trim the bushes, and use the Weed Eater around the house and backyard fence. Though I am tired when I am finished, it feels good seeing how nice things look. I feel much better going to bed at night after accomplishing something.

Moreover, the harder and more difficult the work, the greater sense of accomplishment we feel. Climbing the tallest mountain in Arkansas, Mount Nebo, is not the same as reaching the top of Mount Everest. Though it may be more difficult to live a disciplined life, it will certainly be more rewarding than living a life of ease. This is why we are not to labor halfheartedly, but work with all our might (Eccl. 9:10; Col. 3:23).

One of the most therapeutic things depressed people can do is get their minds off themselves and their problems and begin working hard to take care of themselves and those in need. My friend who watched television all day never heeded my counsel. She never went outside to exercise, she never attempted to reconcile with her family, and she never sought to live for something greater than the moment. Thus, she remained not only stuck in her chair but also stuck in her misery.

There are many good callings in life, such as being a farmer, a construction worker, a business owner, or a house-wife, but any labor that is not done for the glory of God is labor that will be wasted. Even if our work benefits others after we're dead and gone, sooner or later this world will be destroyed—and only that which was done for Christ will last.

A life that falls short of God's glory is a wasted life. It is true, in one sense, that every life is priceless. Being made in the image of God elevates human life, but this intrinsic value is what makes a wasted life all the more sinful. If we do not live for God, then our intrinsic value is wasted. Like a person born into wealth who dies in bankruptcy, those who do not live for God's glory are less than worthless, and it would have been better had they never been born (Matt. 26:24).

Looking for Meaning in What We Possess

If we do not live for the approval of God, we will be left to seek the approval of this world (John 12:42–43). Again, we will seek some type of affirmation. This is not a bad thing, but once we do not care about pleasing God, then we will be forced to look for approval elsewhere.

Rejection and disapproval hurt, which is why it is easy to succumb to peer pressure. We love the praise of people because we want to feel important—for who doesn't like to be liked? Who doesn't want to be appreciated? I know I do. We are tempted to keep up with the Joneses because we are concerned about the opinions of others. Because we envy others who have cool stuff, we assume others will envy us if we have cool stuff. Therefore, we can feel better about ourselves if we think other people are envious of us.

Consequently, our yearning for some materialistic thing is often motivated by our desire to obtain the approval of others. Car manufacturers understand the psychology of this very well. The objective of almost every car commercial is to stir up discontent by leading us to imagine the satisfaction of showing off our new ride to others. Commercials focus on the neighbors' jealousy rather than the new car owner's joy. This type of marketing works, for who doesn't like to buy things to show them off to others?

We are often tempted to think that buying expensive things gives our life greater value. The more our net worth, the more our self-worth—or so the thinking goes. This is the reason so many of us place our identity in the car we drive. It is easier to sit up straighter when others notice we're driving a new SUV. And if we cannot afford a new vehicle, then we are tempted to place our self-worth in a pair of designer jeans.

Yet the glory of this world is fading away. Does a luxury SUV have greater eternal value than a beat-up station wagon from the used car lot? Is a new pair of designer jeans worth more eternally than worn-out ones from the local thrift shop? No, in the end, after we are dead, the kind of car we drove or the jeans we strutted will not matter.

The Lord Jesus warned us to "take heed and beware of covetousness, for one's life does not consist in the abundance of the things he possesses" (Luke 12:15). For instance, a young Scottish girl named Jane Parks won a million euros with a lottery ticket and thought she was extremely lucky. Yet four years later—after buying her own house, a purple Range Rover, and a pet Chihuahua—she explained:

> At times it feels like winning the lottery has ruined my life. I thought it would make my life ten times better but it's made it ten times worse. I wish I had no money most days.
>
> I say to myself, "My life would be so much easier if I had not won." People look at me and think, "I wish I had her lifestyle, I wish I had her money." But they do not realize the extent of my stress. I have material things but apart from that my life is empty. What is my purpose in life?[1]

Jane Parks is a living illustration of how "one's life does not consist in the abundance of the things he possesses" (Luke 12:15).

Seeking glory, happiness, and identity in the things we possess leaves us feeling empty. As soon as we place our hope in perishable things, we cannot help but realize that our glory, happiness, and identity are perishing too. No matter how expensive the house, the car, or the jeans, we cannot help but know that they are a cheap substitute for the eternal glory that can be found only in God.

Looking for Meaning in Who We Are

To gain self-worth and glory, we are tempted to think we need some form of external verification. And if we cannot find it in what we do or what we possess, then we will try to find it in who we are. We go from looking for value in

---

1. Catriona Harvey-Jenner, "A 17-Year-Old Girl Won the Lottery, But Says It 'Ruined Her Life,'" Yahoo! Lifestyle, accessed February 15, 2017, https://www.yahoo.com/style/17-old-girl-won-lottery-133614023.html.

what we do and what we possess to looking for value for just being alive.

Like Narcissus who fell in love with himself after seeing his reflection in a pool of water, we are tempted to look for purpose and identity in the superficial reflection of our own image. Rather than loving others as we love ourselves, we want others to love us as we love ourselves. We find ourselves thinking, "As charming and good looking as I am, I should not have to climb Mount Everest to be praised. Why should I have to do anything important to feel important? Just being me should be enough to cause the whole world to appreciate me. Doesn't God love me just as I am? I know I do!"

So we go from wanting to work hard at doing something great to working hard promoting ourselves without doing anything worthwhile. But no one likes a pompous person, so we have learned the art of bringing attention to ourselves without sounding like we are bragging. It is not vain to post a selfie if we add a "blessed" hashtag. It is not self-praise when we retweet the good things other people say about us. This type of self-promotion attracts attention, and this superficial praise is addicting. Once we get even a tiny spotlight shining on us, it is hard to step back into the shadows of obscurity.

It is easy to become dependent on the attention we receive through social media. We are eager to share every little event in our life, thinking that the world is dying to know that we ate lunch at Torchy's Tacos. What started as a profile picture has turned into a weekly or even daily selfie. And if today's selfie does not get the same number of "likes" as yesterday's, then we feel disappointed—somehow our self-worth has been tarnished a bit.

Sadly, when we have no real purpose in life, this is what it comes down to—seeking superficial verification without doing anything worthy of praise. We continue to seek some type of approval because subconsciously we know we are wasting our lives and do not feel good about who we are.

Purpose Is Found Only in God

Yet even if we received the approval of the whole world, what lasting value does this give us? Do we think people in hell are praising each other? Do we believe winning the Nobel Peace Prize would be of any lasting consolation? Do we really suppose our value is determined by the silly and fickle opinions of others?

Needing affirmation is not the problem, however. In fact, God has placed this need within us. We need approval, but we were designed by God to seek His approval, and only His approval can give our lives any lasting value. Seeking value in the things we possess is also not a problem if we are seeking to possess Christ. If we possess Christ, we possess all things. Because we have been "blessed with every spiritual blessing in the heavenly places in Christ," it is true that Jesus plus nothing equals everything (Eph. 1:3).

We do not have to find glory in our self-worth or in materialistic things that are perishing. Custom-fitted suits and expensive jewelry are nice, but they are worthless in bestowing any true honor and value. Real value—the unadulterated glory we long for—comes only from knowing God. It is one thing to say, "I own a pair of Air Jordan IVs" but quite another thing to say, "I belong to God, and He belongs to me." To know God—to be His friend—is truly something to glory in, for it is the only thing that brings us true identity and purpose (Ps. 62:7). Likewise, this glory is found only when we do not glory in ourselves, but in Christ (1 Cor. 1:31). As God says, "Let him who glories glory in this, that he understands and knows Me" (Jer. 9:24).

Living for the glory of God gives peasants eternal value while living for the glory of self devalues even the lives of kings. Only living for Christ will give us true purpose. Even little tasks, such as sweeping the kitchen floor, take on an eternal value when they are done to please God (Eph. 6:6).

Even though you might not be the CEO of a Fortune 500 company, your calling is noble when you carry it out in a way that brings honor and glory to God. Even eating and drinking, when done with thankfulness to God, will bring you eternal glory (1 Cor. 10:31). Though a housewife may feel unnoticed by the world, though she may feel unappreciated by her own family, and though she may feel she is of little value to the kingdom of God, her life has real and lasting significance when she seeks to do everything for the glory of God. Those who are first in this life, such as the famous movie star, shall be last, and those who are last, such as the obscure housewife, shall be first in the life to come (Matt. 20:16).

Moreover, God will not forget one cup of cold water given in the name of the Lord (Matt. 10:42). Every good work will follow us into eternity (Rev. 14:13). What we give away in this life will be given back to us in the next life. The Lord has a book of remembrance that contains every virtuous deed we have done, no matter how small. Even what would seem to be the most insignificant thing, such as a quick thought about God, will be forever remembered by Him (Mal. 3:16).

The woman with the alabaster jar did not waste her precious perfume when she broke the jar and anointed Christ's head (Matt. 26:7). Rather, her sacrificial act will forever be remembered and appreciated by the Lord (Matt. 26:13). Likewise, *everything* has eternal value when it is carried out for the glory of God. Now this, and this alone, brings us purpose.

Conclusion

Even now, in this life, we can live for eternity. We can invest in the world to come by laying up for ourselves treasures in heaven. We do not have to be a foreign missionary to live for the glory of God. We simply seek to do the little things with a heart of love and thankfulness to God.

This brings us purpose, meaning, value, and identity. In fact, this is the only way for us *not* to waste our lives. Our lives begin to be meaningful when they are surrendered to the Lord, and they continue to be meaningful as we find our greatest joy in seeking to glorify Christ with every thought and deed. Purpose comes by us living for eternity. Though living for Christ may not garner people's praise, and though we may even be hated and despised by the world, it will all be worthwhile when we hear our precious Savior say, "Well done, good and faithful servant" (Matt. 25:21). Until then, we live with purpose. We live to please our Lord. We live to enjoy and glorify God in all that we possess, all that we do, and all that we are. This, and this alone, is a life worth living.

⚶ QUESTIONS FOR REFLECTION

1. Why is working important?

2. Why are we tempted to look for purpose in the things we possess?

3. Why is vain to seek purpose in glorifying ourselves?

4. Why is our purpose found only in glorifying God?

4

the pursuit of *Freedom*

A few years ago I visited the Medieval Crime Museum in Rothenburg, Germany. Of all the torture devices on display that were designed to slowly inflict excruciating pain on its victims, the one that stood out to me the most was the Iron Maiden. An evil mind must have taken counsel from the devil in a very dark age to devise such a wicked apparatus. It is a single-hinged iron cabinet, shaped like an Egyptian mummy sarcophagus, with a spike-covered interior.

Could you imagine being squeezed into one of these contraptions for any extended period of time? The initial terror of hundreds of spikes penetrating your body would be miserable enough. But once you were locked in, how could you bear not being able to move a single muscle? How could you handle being stuck standing still in the same position for days? Your feet would begin to grow tired even after the first few hours. If you tried to relax and rest your weight, you would only be forcing the spikes to penetrate deeper into your body. To relinquish the pain, the knee-jerk reaction would be to shift your weight in the other direction. But this too would only cause you to feel the knife-like incisions on the other side of your body.

The mental frustration would be as torturous as the physical pain. The impulse to squirm and flail your arms and legs would be constant. You would know you needed to remain completely still, but the inside of you would be dying to thrash around like a madman. Under such confinement, you would begin to cry out: "Let me out of here! Let me out of here! Let me out of here!" But confined you would remain— with no certainty that you would ever be released.

Such confinement is the epitome of torture. This is because inside us all is the innate desire to be free. We all want to be free. The little boy or girl inside us longs to run loose in an open field with hands up in the air shouting, "I am *f-r-e-e-e-e-e-e*!"

This pursuit of freedom is in us all because we are made in the image of God. We long for the glory of being free to do only what we want to do, when we want to do it. We do not want anything binding our wills. This is the freedom we all desire.

Freedom Is Not Found in Lawlessness

The Bible tells us, however, that our wills are born enslaved to sin (Eph. 2:1–4). Sin is enslaving by its very nature (John 8:34). It binds us like an Iron Maiden, but it is much crueler than any man-made torture device. Unlike the Iron Maiden, sin promises us freedom and delivers a short burst of pleasure only to pierce our lives with unending torment as it tightens its grip more securely around our souls.

We are all born with a sinful nature that deceives us into thinking freedom is found in fulfilling the desires of our flesh. If we are going to be free, we often think to ourselves, then our appetites, desires, wants, and cravings need to be unleashed without any restrictions. To be free, we need no laws, no rules, no oversight, no accountability, and no conscience binding our wills. We need to be able to dive in and pig out without being told no. Self must be uninhibited to do what it wants if we are going to be free. This is the type of freedom that sin promises us.

"No one is going to tell me what to do" is the attitude of so many people. In high school I had a friend who had this very mind-set. No one could control him, not even his mother. I remember at a basketball game he asked his mother for five dollars so he could buy some cheese nachos at the concession stand. She told him something he did not want to hear: no. Yet no was not an option for him. He raised his eyebrows and responded sharply: "You do not want me to cause a scene, *do you*?" She then bowed her head in defeat, reached into her purse, and handed over the money to her bratty son.

Apparently, my friend's mother had lost control of him prior to this shameful episode. And by the time he was in high school, he couldn't even control himself. Though he was one of the best basketball players on the team, he stormed off and quit during practice because he could not stand to be corrected by the coach. As you could imagine, he did not have the self-control to graduate and, as far as I know, was never able to hold down a job. Unfortunately, he was tragically killed in a car accident a few years after I last heard from him.

In pursuing this kind of freedom, many are deceived by living only for the moment. Like wild animals that cannot think beyond their current impulse, they live only to satisfy their felt needs. They are compelled to do whatever is most pleasing for the moment, no matter what the cost. Like a stream of water flowing downhill, they always take the path of least resistance.

For instance, I helped create a budget for a lady who had no self-control. Month after month she would frivolously spend her entire disability check the day it came in the mail. Afterward she would complain that she had no money for rent or groceries. So after allotting the amount she needed for her bills, there was enough remaining for her to receive a thirty-dollar weekly allowance. And it was not long before she began to ask for her allowance early. On one particular occasion she asked for it early so she could buy a slushy. Feeling a little contrary, I gave her an option, "Would you rather receive twenty dollars today or wait and get the full thirty dollars tomorrow?"

She responded as if it were a no-brainer: "I would rather have twenty dollars today."

Even after I explained that the slushy would cost her an extra ten dollars, she said she did not care. Then I thought I would make it a little more difficult. "Would you rather have ten dollars today or wait and receive the full amount tomorrow?"

Again, she quickly answered, "I would rather have the ten dollars now."

Being astonished with her lack of self-control, I asked, "What about five dollars today, or wait and get the full thirty dollars tomorrow?"

She must have wanted that slushy badly because she answered, "I will take the five dollars."

Though this sounds ridiculous, many of us cannot boast of being much wiser than the slushy lady, for we are up to our eyeballs in credit card debt. We cannot wait to have the new television and the latest technological gadgets right now. It doesn't matter if we can't afford it, as long as we get our "slushy."

With a credit card in hand, we easily think that we have the freedom to buy what we want when we want it. Yet is the freedom to indulge the flesh true freedom? Does living for the moment—doing what our five senses tell us to do—really liberate us? No! Though indulging our flesh is fun, it only brings us into deeper slavery. As with the prodigal son, we so often sabotage tomorrow's happiness to have a few moments of temporary pleasure.

Consequently, if we cannot submit to authority, it is because we have no authority and control over ourselves. Apart from God, our wills are bound to our fleshly desires. We may think we are free, but it is evident that we are enslaved to our own self-destructive passions, which are driving us. It may be an addiction to drugs, alcohol, sex, money, or buying cool stuff, but whatever it is, our passions turn us about like a leaf blown aimlessly in the air.

The selfish nature with which we were born dictates that we please our flesh, but our flesh is a cruel taskmaster. "There is no slavery so base," according to Henry Scougal, "as that whereby we become a mindless drone to our own lusts."[1] No matter how hard we seek to satisfy our passions, they are never satisfied. We will always want more; there is never enough. Our passions continue to demand more than the world can supply. Like a blazing fire, the more we feed our flesh, the more it consumes us.

---

1. Scougal, *Life of God in the Soul of Man*, 58.

Selfishness is not only insatiable but also highly deceptive. No matter how much we seek to fulfill our lusts, we continue to be tricked into thinking that we need just a little bit more to be happy. We are almost there—we are so close that we can taste it. Like a dog chasing its tail, we continue to go around and around, pursuing what is always alluding us. So we continue to serve our flesh—our master—while being pulled into deeper and deeper bondage. It is as though we are wearing Chinese handcuffs—the more we seek to squirm free, the more the restraints pull us into captivity.

The foolishness of it all is that we serve self willingly. We do not mind digging our own grave because we are deceived into thinking freedom and happiness lay at the bottom of the pit. But the hole we have dug is now the hole that enslaves us. By loving sin, we are embracing the poisonous snake that is biting us. The thing that is robbing us of freedom is the very thing we think we must have to be free. This is the deception of sin—it causes us to live for the thing that is killing us.

In other words, we are bound to our own selfishness. Our wills are bound to obey the lusts of our flesh; that is, according to Jonathan Edwards, our will is free only to choose according to our strongest desire.[2] And our strongest desires are determined by the nature of our hearts. Because we are born with a sinful heart, our wills are enslaved to our own sinful motives. As long as we are outside of Christ and our wills are bound to the sinful desires of our heart, we will have no control over our own feelings. So when we are controlled

---

2. Jonathan Edwards, *The Freedom of the Will* (Morgan, Pa.: Soli Deo Gloria Publications, 1996), 5–15.

by our insatiable passions, we cannot help but be enslaved to our emotions.

The problem is that our sinful hearts have strong cravings that are never satisfied. James 4:2 says that sinful hearts "lust and do not have. [They] murder and covet and cannot obtain. [They] fight and war." Thus, the emotional frustration of never being satisfied fills us with the works of the flesh, such as envy, bitterness, anger, anxiety, depression, and every other emotional annoyance (Gal. 5:19–21). The lack of peace and satisfaction fills us with every bitter emotion, tossing us about like a little rowboat lost at sea.

Therefore, we have emotional problems because we always want what we cannot obtain. The truth be told, we want to control everything. This is the "freedom" that our depraved nature seeks. In fact, the selfish heart, because of its very nature, wants to be god. I do not mean selfishness wants to be the God of the universe. We are even too selfish to want to take care of everything. What is taking place on the other side of the world does not concern us much. Let God take care of all the things we do not care about. But in our selfishness, we just want to be god over self and all the things that are connected to or could possibly interfere with self.

If it is natural for us to want our way, then we naturally want to make sure nothing interferes with our getting what we want. Again, this is why we get so frustrated, angry, sad, depressed, or jealous with circumstances and with people who oppose us.

Up and down we go, around and around, as we are blown about by the good or bad circumstances that lie outside our control. Without self-control, we are "like a city broken down, without walls" (Prov. 25:28). Any little thing can penetrate and make us miserable. And here lies the problem with being enslaved to our emotions—our emotions become controlled by various external circumstances that we have no power to control. Though we may desire to control the various circumstances that interfere with our lives, the reality is that we know we cannot control these things. We may be depressed about the past, but this is something we cannot change. We may be anxious about the future, but this, too, is out of our control.

What can we control then? The only things we are responsible to control are how we think, feel, and behave at this present moment. This is the limited extent of our power. You can choose to continue reading or to stop reading this book. Maybe you could throw this book in the trash, but you cannot choose to fly to the moon or eliminate all your problems with the snap of your fingers. Almost everything you and I want to control are things that only God can control. Thus, many of our emotional problems occur when we bump up against the reality that we are not God. This happens almost every day. It is the frustration we feel when we realize that we do not have the freedom we think we should have.

Our fleshly nature does not want to submit everything, such as our finances, our careers, our health, our families, and our destinies, to the rule and sovereignty of God. We have a hard time trusting God with the things we care about. We think we know better than God. We worry that God may make a mistake. So we complain, grumble, and get bitter with the trials of life. Like bratty children, we get all worked up when we think we are not going to get our way.

But the worst of it is that we are allowing the things we cannot control, such as the past or the future, to control the only thing we are responsible to control—our present thoughts, feelings, and actions. In other words, we lose control of the things we are responsible to control by wanting to control the things outside our control.

This was the case with a man I once counseled who was terrified to leave his apartment. He had an unreasonable fear of the outdoors. Even getting his mail was something that scared him. Inside his apartment he felt comfortable—as if he were in control. But outside the protection of those walls, he felt as if anything could happen. There were too many unknown variables for him to feel secure. He was fearful of the things outside his control. What a hindrance this was to him. He felt he could not work. He would not even buy groceries. His emotions enslaved him to his one-bedroom apartment.

Like this man, many of us are allowing things outside our control to control the things we are responsible to control. How often have we neglected our responsibilities because we did not feel like doing them? We procrastinate because we do not feel like turning off the television and getting off the couch. How often have we spoken in anger because it felt good? In the end, by seeking the freedom to indulge our flesh, we become emotionally enslaved to the various circumstances that are outside our power.

Freedom Is Not Found in the Law
To find true freedom, however, we must gain control over our emotions. It is one thing to have the political freedom to live our lives in the way we believe is best, but it is another thing to have the volitional freedom to be able to do what is best. What good is it to have freedom from external suppression if

we are the ones suppressing ourselves? It is of little value to win the battle if we are going to defeat ourselves afterward.

This is why those who rule over their emotions have more freedom in prison than do selfish kings who rule over nations. Though Paul was a prisoner of the Roman emperor Nero, it was Paul who enjoyed true freedom. Nero lost himself in his madness and was driven to suicide while Paul had learned the secret to contentment in any circumstance (Phil. 4:11–12). For this reason, those of us who rule over our emotions are better than those who rule over a city (Prov. 16:32).

To gain freedom—true freedom—we must gain control over our emotions. But to gain control over our emotions, we must gain control over our selfish passions and sinful nature. We need something other than our fleshly passions to rule over us because the things of this world are perishing. If our hearts are fixed on something that is constantly in motion, our emotions will be constantly in motion as well. Our feelings need to be anchored to something secure—something that does not move.

Thus, our emotions must be ruled by the truth. This is why God has given us His immutable law to guide our thoughts, emotions, and wills. If we are depressed and cannot get out of bed, the worst thing we can do is obey our feelings. Staying in bed may be the easiest thing to do, but it will only compound our problems. Not only will we be depressed but we will be depressed over being depressed. By staying in bed we're allowing the things outside our control to control the one thing we're responsible to control—getting out of bed and going to work. What must we do? We must do what is right, regardless of how we feel. It may have to start with moving one leg at a time, but we must not allow ourselves the option to stay in bed and wallow in our misery.

Likewise, we must be committed to obey God regardless of how we feel. Being responsible means being faithful, in spite of our circumstances. We must pray even when we do not feel spiritual (1 Thess. 5:17). We must trust God even when we feel like He has abandoned us. We must love our spouses even when they are being hateful.

There is never justification to do evil. Just because someone is hostile to us does not give us the right to cease to obey God. We are even called to love our enemies and pray for those who spitefully use us (Matt. 5:44). We are called to do what is right in a world that is full of wrong.

If our emotions rule over us because of our selfishness, then to be free we must refrain from obeying our sinful passions. If transgression against God's law brings us into slavery, then obedience to God's law is the way out. In this sense, the law works as a boundary marker separating the realm of freedom from the realm of slavery. In sum, if we want to be free, we must submit ourselves to God's boundary marker— His law.

Freedom Is Found Only in Christ

Even with the knowledge of God's law, however, our problem remains. Though the law can point us to freedom, it does not have the power to deliver us from the bondage of sin. This is because the law in and of itself is not sufficient to change our hearts. If we obey only out of obligation, we have yet to obey at all. If we obey God only to avoid negative consequences or to gain some reward, our motives come short of the law's demands. If our motives are selfish, then we have come short of obeying the law that forbids selfishness.

To be free to obey God, we must enjoy and delight in obeying God. To obey God, we must truly, from our heart, love God and love our neighbors as ourselves. Otherwise, in our attempt to obey, our wills, affections, and passions are not acting freely. We are truly free only when we want, love, desire, enjoy, and delight in obeying God. Yet it is only when we enjoy obeying God that we are free to do what we want to do. When we want to obey God because we really do love God, then we are free indeed (1 John 5:3).

And this is why we need Christ in order to be free. We need supernatural deliverance from sin and from ourselves. We cannot change our desires any more than a leopard can change its spots (Jer. 13:23). To be free, we need the love of God to be poured out into our hearts. We need a heart transplant and a new nature. We need new affections, new passions, and new values. We need true repentance and hatred toward sin. We need that which only Christ can give us—we need to be born again (John 3:3). And this is why we need Christ!

Christ said, "Most assuredly, I say to you, whoever commits sin is a slave of sin. And a slave does not abide in the house forever, but a son abides forever. Therefore if the Son makes you free, you shall be free indeed" (John 8:34–36). Only Christ can crucify our old man and its self-guided passions. Only Christ can deliver us from ourselves. Not until our old self is crucified with Christ will we be free from sin. As it is written: "For he who has died has been freed from sin" (Rom. 6:7).

It is true that we will have to wait until we get to heaven before we no longer struggle with the passions of our flesh. It is only when we are glorified that we will no longer need any external law telling us what to do, for then we will only do what we want to do. Until then, we who believe in Christ will continue to war with the desires of our flesh (Gal. 5:17). Yet we do not have to feel conquered, for we can do all things through Christ who strengthens us (Phil. 4:13). By faith in Christ, we have the freedom to say no to sin. We do not have to obey the lusts of the flesh (Rom. 6:12).

In Christ we are free to present ourselves "to God as being alive from the dead" (Rom. 6:13). We are free to present our members to God as instruments for righteousness. We are free to walk in the Spirit (Gal. 5:16). As the Scriptures say:

> There is therefore now no condemnation to those who are in Christ Jesus, who do not walk according to the flesh, but according to the Spirit. For the law of the Spirit of life in Christ Jesus has made me free from the law of sin and death. For what the law could not do in that it was weak through the flesh, God did by sending His own Son in the likeness of sinful flesh, on account of sin: He condemned sin in the flesh, that the righteous requirement of the law might be fulfilled in us who do not walk according to the flesh but according to the Spirit. For those who live according to the flesh set their minds on the things of the flesh, but those who live according to the Spirit, the things of the Spirit. For to be carnally minded is death, but to be spiritually minded is life and peace. Because the carnal mind *is* enmity against God; for it is not subject to the law of God, nor indeed can be. So then, those who are in the flesh cannot please God.

But you are not in the flesh but in the Spirit, if indeed
the Spirit of God dwells in you. Now if anyone does not
have the Spirit of Christ, he is not His. (Rom. 8:1–9)

Thus, true freedom is found in Christ. It comes by pick-
ing up our cross daily and crucifying the desires of the flesh
(Luke 9:23), by laying aside the cares of this world and besetting sins that so easily entangle us (Heb. 12:1), and by being
transformed by the renewing of our minds (Rom. 12:2). Yes,
true freedom comes by seeking first the kingdom of God
(Matt. 6:33), by setting our thoughts and affections on things
above (Col. 3:2), by being spiritually minded (Rom. 8:6), and
by seeing, enjoying, and glorifying God.

Conclusion

If we are seeking freedom by serving the lusts of the flesh,
then we will remain miserably enslaved to our flesh. If we are
living for Twinkies, then all someone has to do to make us
miserable is to steal our Twinkies. Yet if we are storing up our
treasure in heaven and living for the glory of God, then what
can anyone do to take away our joy, purpose, and freedom?
Therefore, the key to having freedom is having a heart that is
fixed on serving our Deliverer.

The Iron Maiden may be able to enslave the body, but sin
enslaves the soul. The torture of the Iron Maiden extends only
to this life, but the torture of sin extends to the life to come
for eternity. People in hell will still be hungry and thirsty, but
they will not be able to enjoy a single moment of pleasure.
They will experience uncontrolled lusts with absolutely no
fulfillment. With such inner torment, the emotional agony
will rule over them with despair, hopelessness, bitterness,

anger, rage, depression, and every other vile feeling. And this is forever in an inescapable pit of fire!

We long for true freedom. We long for our affections, emotions, and wills to be absolutely free. True freedom comes only by letting go of this world. We must die to self before we can live for the glory of God (Matt. 10:39). We must be willing to forsake our life to find life. We must turn over our rights to find freedom. We must have a new nature that is controlled by love before we can be free of the bondage of sin. Glorious and unadulterated freedom may be had, but we must become a slave to Christ (Rom. 6:22).

৯ QUESTIONS FOR REFLECTION

1. Why do lawlessness and sin lead to captivity?

2. Why is it important to rule over our emotions?

3. Why is the law powerless to provide us with emotional freedom?

4. Why is freedom found only in Christ?

the pursuit of Companionship

Alone I traveled across Europe. I was a single college graduate looking for an adventure. With a backpack and a few bucks in hand, I saw castles and cathedrals in Germany, visited famous monuments and museums in Paris, ate waffles and chocolate in Belgium, and got lost for hours walking around in the middle of the night in Zurich. It was great! In all these places, however, I felt the loneliest not when I had lost my way in Zurich, a large, unknown city where I could not speak the language, but when I saw the grandeur of the Swiss Alps for the first time.

Eventually I did find my hostel in Zurich, and the next morning I traveled by train south into the heart of Switzerland. I journeyed through miles of rolling hills that were covered with the greenest grass I had ever seen, dotted with cottages, milk cows, and farms. No doubt the milk from those cows was being turned into Swiss cheese as I zipped past them. Everything looked so beautiful. Soon the rolling hills started to grow larger and larger. The train tracked up and then down and then back up again. Grass-covered hills began to expand into small mountains, and small mountains began to be overcome by larger ones covered with lush pastures until the mountains were so large the green grass grew into giant fir trees.

My face was glued to the window, for I was scared to blink unless I might miss something—such as one of the many snow-fed waterfalls cascading down the mountains. The train continued to climb in elevation until the snow-covered rocks and cliffs left the trees behind. The higher the train scaled, the deeper the valleys grew. And then the moment happened that I would never forget. As the train clung to the side of a mountain, a panoramic view suddenly opened up into the valley below where I beheld the most beautiful place in the world—Interlaken.

Interlaken, as its name suggests, is a resort town that is nestled between two pristine lakes, Thun and Brienz. Like armed guards, the Bernese Oberland Alps surround the picturesque town below. With the clear, blue sky above and the vistas of the snow-capped mountains surrounding the valley, I could not believe my eyes. It was spectacular! The lake water was glacier blue—the bluest of blues. No matter what direction I looked, it was breathtaking. I did my best to stamp the image into my mind, for I knew my camera was incapable of capturing the glory of it all. Amazed, yet I felt alone.

As the train made its descent to its final destination, I felt something was missing. There was an emptiness I could not ignore. Though I was having a blast, I kept thinking about my parents. I could not get them off my mind. "I wish they were here," I thought to myself. "Oh, my dad would love this. I wish my mom could see this." Being single, I always felt a little lonely, but in that moment the feeling was amplified. Such beauty is not meant to be experienced alone. I could not help but want to share the experience with someone—anyone.

Like hitting a hole-in-one when no one is looking, something is not right about seeing the Alps for the first time by yourself. God did not design us to experience life alone (Gen. 2:18). We crave sharing our time, our joys, our sorrows, our hopes, our dreams, and our lives with those we love. We need to love and to be loved. We need friendship. We are relational beings.

Complete isolation is not natural. Because of our innate emptiness and sense of loneliness, we cannot help but crave companionship. Being made in God's image, we were made for relationships. But we were not merely designed for human relationships; we were designed for something much greater. We were designed to participate in the joy that is shared between the Father, the Son, and the Holy Spirit.

A relationship with God, however, has been severed by disobedience. When Adam and Eve fell into sin, not only did they have their first domestic dispute but they and God no longer enjoyed each other's company. Adam and Eve's relationship with God was broken. After they hid from God, God forced them out of His presence (Gen. 3:22–24). Because of the now-broken relationship, humanity has been looking, longing, and searching for that which sin has ruined—perfect companionship.

Companionship Is Not Found in Selfishness

Sin, by its nature, destroys relationships. Coming from a heart of selfishness, sin is the reason our relationships are less than ideal. Because of selfishness, we are prone to sacrifice our relationships for personal gain. So often our career, our hobbies, or our favorite sports teams have caused us to push God, family, and friends aside. Throughout many years of providing marriage counseling, I have seen the terrible effects that sin has on the family. At the heart of all marriage conflict is self-centeredness. Lack of communication, anger, separate bedrooms, infidelity, divorce, and other such marital problems can be traced back to husbands and wives being pulled away from each other by their own self-interests.

For eight consecutive weeks I counseled a man who seemed to have everything. It appeared that each week he was driving a different luxury vehicle. As I was sitting across from him, I couldn't help but notice how cuff links and a precision haircut take the professional look to a whole new level. He looked important and wealthy because he was important and wealthy.

Though he seemed to have everything, he came to me for help. I remember when he looked at me with such apprehension and said, "Jeff, I have been promoted to vice president of a Fortune 500 company, and I am making unbelievable money." Then he went on to explain the amazing opportunities that such an income was providing for him and his family. Though I am not sure of the amount, I would not be surprised if it was close to a million dollars a year. Yet after building the case for why he was so fortunate to have such a coveted position, he said, "But the pressure of my job is consuming me. I am always out of town, flying from city to city. I barely see my children. And my wife wants a divorce. Jeff, what do I do?"

After taking a breath, I answered, "Quit your job!" His eyes grew larger, as if he could not believe what I had just said. But I went on to say, "You are selling out your relationships with your wife and children for professional advancement. Of course you may think you can have them both, but it is your family that is paying the price. Your job has become more important to you than your family. I know it would be hard to turn your back on such wealth," I went on to explain, "but you have to decide which you love more—your career or your family."

After a few moments of silence, as if he were contemplating things, he confessed, "I have sought counsel from multiple colleagues and friends, and you are the only one to tell me that I need to quit my job." After pausing for a second, he went on to say, "But I know you're right."

Think about it with me. What if you had the option to live anywhere, such as Interlaken, Switzerland, and become the richest person in the world? I am talking about unlimited buying power. Mansions, yachts, a private island, a fleet of private jets, every exotic sports car, and every other imaginable thing that could be bought with money—all available to you, but with one condition. To gain such wealth you have to trade in your relationships—all of them. To gain such wealth, you could not maintain any relationships with your parents, your siblings, your spouse, your children, or your friends. You would even have to give up your dog, Fido.

Of course you would have millions of admirers. You would have lots of people *pretending* to be your friends. Everyone would want to hang out with you and enjoy your cool stuff, but you would know that they only liked you for your stuff.

Would you exchange your relationships and friends for wealth? Everyone I have ever presented this hypothetical scenario to has said no. When we think deeply about it, we know relationships are more important than money and earthly success.

Our best memories—the memories we would be devastated to lose—are those that include other people. Looking back, what made Christmas so great were not the toys as much as it was family. Remembering the times Mom made cookies and Dad dressed up like Santa means more to us now than the presents did then. Family vacations were great because our parents taught us how to put up a tent and build a campfire. The memories of building forts or having tea parties are special because our siblings, cousins, and friends were a vital part of our childhood.

It is family and friends who make this life so special. Evidently our happiness, purpose, and even freedom, which we have looked at in the previous chapters, are to be found in relationships. Take relationships away from life, and life becomes miserable and meaningless.

Yet you and I so often place self-interest, personal pleasure, and our career above the people we care about the most. We do not have time to play football with our sons outside the house because we are too busy watching football by ourselves inside the house. We miss out on watching our children grow up because we are too concerned about building our portfolios. We would rather use video games and day care to raise our children than sacrifice our careers.

Quality time dedicated to strengthening our marriages is becoming a thing of the past because of the additional pressures we have taken on at work. We need the money, right? We do not know how to say no to things—even good things—that pull our affections away from the people we love. Busy, busy, busy we have become.

What must we do? We must protect our relationships. We must keep our devotion time with the Lord. Prayer, Bible intake, and Christian fellowship are vital. We must make our family a priority. We must make our church family a priority. Relationships require the most important resource we have—our time. We must guard it. We must invest our time in the things that matter most—God, family, and friends.

"I don't know if I have time for all that," you may be thinking. But if you discovered a reservoir of gold in your backyard, suddenly you would find time to start digging. You probably wouldn't even rest until every ounce was mined. Yet the real gold is the passing and unrecoverable moments we could spend with the ones we love. If we could just realize the value of spending quality time with the Lord and with our loved ones, then we would not be so eager to waste our time digging for the gold that perishes.

Companionship Is Not Found in Lust

Relationships require time, but what they need most is love (1 John 4:8). Without love, relationships will deteriorate into selfish people exploiting each other for their personal gain. Because relationships require love, God has given us His law so that we will know what it means to love. God's law not only forbids selfish behavior but it commands that we love God with our hearts and love our neighbors as ourselves (Mark 12:30–31). In fact, the totality of God's law can be summarized by the word *love*, as the apostle Paul explains in Romans 13:8: "Owe no one anything except to love one another, for he who loves another has fulfilled the law." For this reason, God's law is not seeking to manipulate our external behavior, as if the goal were to get us to behave like Pharisees. Rather, the objective of His law is to instruct us on how to have a loving relationship with God and how to have loving relationships with others.

The first four commandments of God's law tell us how to maintain a relationship with God, and the next six commandments tell us how to maintain a relationship with others (Ex. 20:3–17). So God's law is principally concerned about relationships. If we miss this, we miss the intent of the law. Since we need relationships and sin destroys relationships, obeying God's law is in our best interest (Luke 10:27). Although making self our top priority may seem to be what is in our best interest, selfishness only undermines our happiness, purpose, and freedom, as we have seen in the past few chapters.

Selfishness is deceptive, however. With the help of Hollywood, it has deceived the world into embracing a counterfeit love. Selfishness has made love into its own image. This cheap knockoff is often identified as love, but it is completely powerless in helping us obey God's law.

This knockoff is a counterfeit that deceives many people because it looks like the real thing. Like love, it is an emotion— often an intense and passionate emotion. Like love, it can also be sacrificial. It will cause people to spend their money, send flowers, open car doors for companions, dedicate their time, and do other such self-giving services. What is this counterfeit love? Its name is lust.

There is one major difference between love and lust, however. The end objective of love is the betterment of others while the end objective of lust is the satisfaction of self. We lust after many things, such as food, clothing, money, romance, and the like. And rather than calling these cravings by their real names, we call them love. Who does not love ice cream sundaes, for instance?

When we are craving ice cream, however, we are not thinking about what is in the best interest of the ice cream. Though this craving produces a strong emotion in us, and though we are willing to sacrifice a few bucks to buy it, we are only thinking about our own desires. We really do not love ice cream sundaes in the truest sense of the word. Instead, we love ourselves. Ice cream is merely a means to please self.

Our culture is so blinded by its own selfishness that the vast number of today's marriages are purchased with this counterfeit currency. "I just love him." "She makes me feel so good when I am around her." "She is so pretty; I cannot stop thinking about her." And for a while, this shared passion between newlyweds will cause husbands and wives to sacrifice for each other. They do not mind buying gifts for one another and exchanging their services to make things work in the home. Indeed, lust can empower marriages for a few years—that is, until all the self-sacrifice is no longer worth it. Lust is not "for better or for worse" but "for better, and it better not get worse."

Marriage is often just a formal agreement to exchange services. People enter into marriages like they enter into a job. Selfish people do not mind working hard as long as there is a paycheck at the end of the day. But few will continue to work for free. Once the romance dies down, once the honeymoon is over, once the beauty begins to fade, once the personal benefits begin to be too expensive, then the relationship begins to deteriorate. Though it was full steam ahead in the beginning, it is hard to keep a marriage running on lust for any extended period of time.

This is because lust is selfish, and selfishness eventually exposes itself for what it really is when things get difficult.

Once the investment outweighs the return, it is hard for selfish husbands and wives to remain committed to each other. They may say that they have fallen out of love, but the truth is that they probably never loved each other in the first place. In fact, lust, if not controlled, has more in common with hate than it does with love. It uses people for personal pleasure and then discharges them into the wastebasket after their resources are all used up.

Companionship in Love
Real love is the opposite. It is so glorious in comparison. Real love is from God (1 John 4:8) and is supernatural because it does not seek its own. As the Scriptures explain: Love suffers long and is kind; love does not parade itself, is not puffed up; does not behave rudely, does not seek its own, is not provoked, thinks no evil; does not rejoice in iniquity, but rejoices in the truth; bears all things, believes all things, hopes all things, endures all things" (1 Cor. 13:4–7). Love truly has the best interest of others in mind (Phil. 2:4) and will sacrifice willingly without seeking anything in return. This is what love is—it gives without seeking to receive (Luke 6:35).

Real love will cause a young husband to remain faithful to his wife even though after she has an accident she will have to live out the rest of her days in a coma. Real love will compel a wife to be kind to an unkind husband. Love can be seen in mothers who get up through the night to feed crying babies. It can be seen in their willingness to sacrifice their personal ambitions and careers to change diapers and clean runny noses. Out of a heart of love, mothers give of themselves day in and day out without a paycheck or much recognition. They will pour themselves into their children, and for what? Are they looking for a huge payday after their children are raised and gone? Are they looking to obtain fame or fortune from all their self-sacrifice? No, the only thing loving mothers desire from all their hard work is the well-being of their children. They just want what's good for their children. The welfare and happiness of their children is their reward. Most vividly, love can be seen by looking at the cross. It was "for the joy that was set before Him"—redeeming His people—that led Christ to willingly endure shame and suffer an excruciating death (Heb. 12:2).

Unlike lust, love does not hurt or shortchange self in the process of self-sacrificing. Lust is self-destructive because it undermines relationships and leads to the misery of loneliness. Lust enslaves self. But love provides us with meaningful relationships and priceless joy. The mother who enjoys seeing her children prosper has all the reward she needs. She is satisfied in knowing her children are blessed. This is a joy that surpasses the temporary pleasure that selfishness provides. A loving mother understands that "it is more blessed to give than to receive" (Acts 20:35).

Love may cause us to lay down our life for our friends (John 15:13), but it will find joy in knowing that our life has benefited the lives of those we love. And this is the nature of love. Love leads us to place our happiness in the happiness of others. Love moves us to share the things we love with the people we love. Love delights in sharing because it delights in bringing joy and blessings to others.

Companionship Is Found in Christ

We not only crave companionship but we crave the love that makes companionship possible. We may think we love our new house, but it does not love us back. Our affection for material things is never reciprocated. We can hug the steering wheel of our new car, but it will never return the embrace.

Moreover, we do not want to be taken advantage of by our friends. We long to be loved and for someone to care about us. We do not want to be exploited; we want to feel cherished. To love someone and to be loved by someone is the most treasured of all blessings. With this in mind, we do not have to be in a good marriage or have healthy earthly relationships to be happy, for even the best earthly relationships fall short of displaying perfect love.

What we need more than anything is the love of God. Only a relationship with God is sufficient because only God's love is perfect. His love is immeasurable and surpasses all understanding (Eph. 3:19). It is a love that gives everything and requires nothing in return (1 Cor. 13:5). It is unconditional (Rom. 5:8) and freely bestowed (1 John 4:10). It is complete and lacks nothing because it is the essence of God Himself (1 John 4:8).

Out of deep love, Christ willingly sacrificed everything to pursue His people. Without any hesitancy, He "made Himself of no reputation, taking the form of a bondservant" (Phil. 2:6–7). Out of love, He gave everything He had—even His own life—to redeem us. It was love that caused Him to endure the shame of the cross (Heb. 12:2). Out of love for us, He was embarrassed, mocked, publicly humiliated, brutally beaten by men, and crushed by His Father (Isa. 53:3–11). He loved us to this extent when we were unlovable (Rom. 5:8).

While we were running away from Him in unrepentance, He came pursuing us until our hearts were subdued to repentance by His love (Rom. 2:4).

And this is the main objective of salvation. Salvation is not principally about being delivered from sin and from the wrath of God, though these things are vital. Rather, the principal purpose of salvation is to reconcile us to God (Eph. 1:10). God redeemed us in Christ to bring us into perfect communion with Him. Sin has destroyed this relationship, so sin had to be conquered for us to have a restored relationship with God. And we are born again by the love of God being poured into our hearts so that we can love and enjoy a relationship with God (Rom. 5:5).

And what a relationship we who are saved have with God! The full inheritance of Christ has been given to us. We are His children (1 John 3:1). We will never lack anything (Rom. 8:32). Now "all things work together for good to those who love God" and "are the called according to His purpose" (Rom. 8:28). And we can be certain that "neither death nor life, nor angels nor principalities nor powers, nor things present nor things to come, nor height nor depth, nor any other created thing, shall be able to separate us from the love of God which is in Christ Jesus our Lord" (Rom. 8:38–39).

This is not all. The love of Christ not only unites us with God but it unites us with His people. We are born into a new family—the family of God. As Christians, we cannot help but want to share our spiritual lives with other believers. The love of God compels us to love the communion of the saints— the church. Carrying out the "one anothers" (Eph. 5:21; Heb. 10:25; 1 Peter 1:22) in the context of a local fellowship of believers is one of the greatest blessings for those who love

God. As relationships are a vital part of our own personal happiness, purpose, and freedom, it is not surprising that salvation brings us into a relationship with the body of Christ. Thus, we can thank God for the fellowship of the saints that He has secured for us in our mutual union in Christ Jesus.

Moreover, we can thank God that heaven is not just an earthly paradise full of sensual pleasures but a place where we can enjoy a perfect and sinless relationship with Christ and His people. Whatever physical enjoyments the eternal state may offer, which will be beyond our imagination, what will make heaven so glorious is the joy of fellowshipping with God and His people in perfect harmony forever. Until then, we are never more like God the Father, who shares His glory and joy with the Son and the Spirit, than when we share the things we love and enjoy, whatever physical, emotional, or spiritual pleasure they may offer, with the ones we love.

Conclusion

Our lives were not designed to be lived alone. We were made to share the life we have with Christ with others. This was made evident to me when I saw the beauty of the Swiss Alps for the first time. As much as I enjoyed experiencing one of the most spectacular places in the universe by myself, such an experience only intensified the incomplete feeling within me.

What a joy it was the next time I visited Switzerland. Traveling with my wife and parents was amazing. I remember feeling a little nervous, however, as the train worked its way into the mountains. I was scared that my parents would be disappointed. I was worried that I may have exaggerated the beauty of the Alps to them. With the passing of time, I was worried that I may have unconsciously embellished the height of the mountains, the depth of the valleys, the blueness of the water, and the overall splendor of everything.

Then the moment happened that made everything feel complete. As the train tracked through the Alps, my mom, with such excitement in her voice, leaned over toward my dad and whispered, "This is the most beautiful place I have ever seen."

My dad replied, "The whole trip is worth it just for this alone."

I asked them if they were in any way disappointed.

"Oh," my mom replied, "you did not even tell us the half of it. This beauty is beyond words."

Seeing my parents' faces light up with joy as they stared out the window—experiencing that moment with them—was a greater delight for me than seeing the scenery passing by outside the window. What makes seeing Switzerland really great is seeing it with the ones you love. There are many blessings to be enjoyed in this world, but it is our relationships that keep these blessings from turning into idols or into curses. Therefore, may we never sacrifice our relationships for empty trinkets or temporary pleasure. Let us make the most of the short time we have on this beautiful planet and give ourselves to loving God with all our hearts and loving our neighbors as ourselves.

♦ QUESTIONS FOR REFLECTION

1. Why is selfishness the enemy of relationships?

2. What is the key difference between love and lust?

3. Why is love so important in relationships?

4. Why is love found only in Christ?

the pursuit of *Truth*

We have a love-hate relationship with truth. On the one hand, we cannot help but pursue it. In our quest for glory, truth is vital. There is no happiness, purpose, freedom, or companionship without truth. On the other hand, apart from God's grace, we stand opposed to the truth that opposes us. We would rather believe a lie than submit to any truth that we consider detrimental to our desire to find happiness, purpose, freedom, and companionship.

The Reasons We Pursue Truth

As a young child I was full of questions. I remember one day in particular that I pestered my dad for hours—hammering him with one question after another—until he kindly bade me stop my relentless inquisition. I understand how he must have felt now that I am father of my own inquisitive children.

Children naturally want to learn. Though some children are not interested in submitting themselves to the rigors of school, they all have certain interests that captivate their curiosity. Some give themselves to academic studies while others spend more time studying how to avoid reading, writing, and arithmetic. But in every case, children are always learning.

We were designed by God to be lifelong students, so a thirst for knowledge is in us all. There is so much we need to know. We have so many questions, and we have questions because there is so much we do not know. Among other things, we want to know who we are, where we come from, where we are going, and what life is all about.

The Reason We Suppress Truth

Sadly, our innate desire to know God and ourselves has been morally impaired by the sin of the first human beings. Adam and Eve were created with a personal knowledge of God, but this knowledge was lost when they rejected the truth by believing the lie of the serpent (Gen. 3:1). Once they rebelled against the truth, they attempted to cover up the truth with a lie—by hiding themselves from God (Gen. 3:8). They wanted to know neither the truth about their sins nor the truth of how God felt about their sins. Out of shame they no longer desired to live in the light. They became lovers of darkness (John 3:19). Since then, all human beings, as descendants of Adam, are born in darkness, having no understanding (Ps. 82:5).

Humankind's inability to understand the truth, according to Jonathan Edwards, is not a physical inability but a moral inability.[1] It is not that sinful people lack the intellectual capacity to grasp the truth; it's that they do not have the moral desire to submit to the truth. Like a panda that has all the physical components to eat meat, natural humans have all the physical tools needed to come to the knowledge of the

---

1. See Edwards, *Freedom of the Will*, 24–31.

truth. Pandas, however, do not like meat. For some strange reason, they like to eat grass. In the same way, natural people do not have an appetite for spiritual truth (1 Cor. 2:14).

People are blind because they do not want to see. As it is impossible for me to enjoy coconut pie, it is impossible for unrepentant sinners to willingly embrace that which they hate. Since people love darkness, they cannot help but hate the light (John 3:19). For this reason unbelievers willfully "suppress the truth in unrighteousness" (Rom. 1:18).

I have seen this type of suppression firsthand. When I was in high school, one of my friends committed suicide. No one saw this coming, especially the boy's mother. I knew denial was one of the steps of grieving but didn't realize how strong this emotion could be. At the graveside, the mother threw herself on top of her son's casket and began to shake it rapidly while crying out, "Wake up, wake up, wake up!" Everyone else stood by silently. Reality was bitter, and in that moment it was too hard for this mother to accept. She, for the time being, would not allow herself to believe her only child was about to be buried. Though the evidence was overwhelming, it was not enough to convince her of something she did not want to believe. Because she loved her son, she did not love the truth.

When truth hurts, we no longer welcome it into our lives. I once talked with a man who was scared to be tested for HIV. He was in the habit of sharing needles with his friends when they shot up drugs and had recently learned that one of these friends tested positive for HIV. He knew this meant there was a possibility he might also have HIV. I encouraged him to be tested, but he said he would rather not know. He thought not knowing was a better option than having to face the possibility that he had an incurable disease.

Sadly, we often believe the light is the problem rather than that we are. If we can push the truth aside, so we think to ourselves, then we can live our lives in peace, as if avoiding being tested for HIV or not thinking about an angry God eliminates the dangers of being infected with a deadly disease or facing God's wrath.

Such a reaction is true for those of us who are unrepentant. As it is not fun for lawbreakers to think about facing a righteous judge, it is not fun for us sinners to think about God. Rather than embracing this knowledge, we, in our instinct for self-preservation, do what we can to push the truth away from our consciences. If we can get rid of our guilt, maybe we can get rid of a righteous God.

By fighting the truth, we are unwittingly fighting ourselves. We cannot help but want to know the truth, as truth is vital for life, but we also struggle to embrace the truth. According to Jonathan Edwards, "Of all the knowledge that we can ever obtain, the knowledge of God, and the knowledge of ourselves, are the most important."[2]

Yet as long as we remain unrepentant, the knowledge of God and of self is the knowledge we hate the most. Though we may want to know, we do not like the truth we uncover. Because a holy God is scary, we would rather believe a lie— any lie—than willingly submit to the truth concerning the depth of our wickedness and of God's holiness.

John Calvin understood that the knowledge of God and the knowledge of self cannot be separated: "Nearly all the

---

2. Edwards, *Freedom of the Will*, xi.

wisdom we possess, that is to say, true and sound wisdom, consists of two parts: the knowledge of God and of ourselves. But, while joined by many bounds, which one precedes and brings forth the other is not easy to discern."[3] This means that when we twist the truth about ourselves, we are forced to twist the truth about God, and vice versa. Since we are made in God's image, the doctrine of God and the doctrine of man stand and fall together. To seek to live peacefully with our guilt, we are tempted to knowingly warp our conception of God and of ourselves.

We are tempted to spin the truth about ourselves. Because we are made in the likeness of a holy God, it is instinctive for us to want to know the truth about ourselves, but because we have been marred into the likeness of fallen man, it is also instinctive for us not to like what we see when we begin our introspection. Those old skeletons need to stay locked up in those dark closets.

Rather than dive too deeply into our consciences and expose all our hidden guilt, we quickly distract our minds by focusing on the few relatively good things we have done. We make excuses for our actions and justify ourselves. We willingly deceive ourselves by thinking we are not all that bad. Before we are finished with our self-evaluation, we puff ourselves up with so much pride that we end up thinking that we are something, when in reality we are nothing (Gal. 6:3). In this way, we willfully blind ourselves to the truth about ourselves.

---

3. John Calvin, *The Institutes of the Christian Religion*, ed. John T. McNeill, trans. Ford Lewis Battles (Philadelphia: Westminster Press, 1977), 1.1.1.

We are also tempted to spin the truth about God. Because God is fearful, we are prone to make God into our own image. We would rather view God as a Santa Claus figure who only wants to bless our lives rather than as a just judge. This is why so many people sit under preachers such as Joel Osteen,[4] who will tell them what they want to hear (2 Tim. 4:3). With a god of their own making, they can feel good about themselves. They might experience a little conviction, but not enough to cause them to utterly deplore themselves. They have done a good job suppressing their guilt through positive thinking, so they need a god that encourages them in their own self-confidence.

Other people think they are too educated to be religious. They are so foolish as to claim that God does not even exist (Ps. 14:1). Whatever lies we may be tempted to believe about God, they are nothing more than our attempts to suppress the guilt we feel when we think about God.

Running away from truth may seem to be the easiest thing to do, but we can never run far enough away. No matter where we seek to hide, the truth is always condemning us (Ps. 19:1–6). The Bible says that we can try to suppress the truth, but it is like holding a beach ball under water; it always wants to spring back up.

---

4. Joel Osteen is a best-selling author and pastor of Lakewood Church, a megachurch in Houston, Texas. Osteen purposefully and admittedly neglects preaching on hell and repentance. See Heather Clark, "Joel Osteen Says He's Not 'Cheating People' by Neglecting to Preach on Repentance, Hell," Christian News Network, March 31, 2016, http://christiannews.net/2016/03/31/joel-osteen-says-hes-not-cheating-people-by-neglecting-to-preach-on-repentance-hell/.

According to the Scriptures, every person knows there is an all-powerful (Rom. 1:20), all-knowing (Acts 17:25), righteous (Ps. 97:6), and angry God (Rom. 1:18) who is going to judge them for their disobedience (Rom. 1:32; 2:15). In essence, their guilt alone leaves them without any excuse.

In short, the reason we refuse the knowledge of a holy God is because we know, deep down, that we are unholy. Yet if we do not want to own up to the full extent of our guilt, we will continue to reject the truth about God. And as long as we refuse the truth, we will remain frustrated in our innate desire to know the truth.

The Reason We Need Truth

Lies and deception have never helped any of us. If we happen to be infected with a deadly disease, it may be easier for the moment to avoid being tested, but sooner or later it is going to catch up with us. What an amazing thought that the majority of people are going to face God unprepared. On the last day, every knee is going to bow to the lordship of Christ (Rom. 14:11). But then it's going to be too late for those who have purposefully suppressed the truth.

Though a guilty conscience is enough to condemn us, it is not sufficient to lead us to repentance. There is no motivation for us to repent if God is bent only on condemning us. If we see only the justice, anger, wrath, and severity of God, we will continue to suppress the knowledge of ourselves and of God (Rom. 1:18). If we think we are doomed, with no hope, we have no motivation to embrace a holy God. We would rather trust in a false hope by grasping after the darkness than expose our evil deeds by coming to the light (John 3:20).

Thankfully, we are not without hope. Though the truth of God's justice will never lead us to repentance, there is more truth about God than justice—the truth of His mercy found in Christ Jesus. Not only is the gospel of the substitutionary death of Christ objectively necessary for us to be justified before God but the gospel message is subjectively necessary for us to willingly embrace the truth about ourselves and about God. It is not until our hearts have recognized God's willingness to forgive us through Christ Jesus that we will ever be moved to willingly embrace the full knowledge of our guilt. When the Spirit effectually shows us Christ hanging on the tree in our place, suddenly God's justice is no longer deplorable (Rom. 2:4). Only when the gospel is illuminated to our hearts are we made willing to embrace the truth about God and ourselves.

By embracing Christ we can embrace the depth of our sins. We can happily accept that we are nothing. It is not until we see Christ that we can see that we are sick and blind and in need of a physician (Mark 2:17). When we see that Christ is a sufficient Savior, we can reject our own righteousness as "filthy rags" (Isa. 64:6). In this sense, only the glory of Christ will fully humble us.

I remember that night I almost committed suicide. Everything was dark, and I was concerned only about myself. Finally, when my dad encouraged me over the phone to pray, I pushed the loaded gun across the floor and determined to seek God until I found relief. I knew something had to give. It was around midnight when I started beseeching God: "Oh, Lord, please take away the pain!" I cried out. I begged and pleaded for hours.

Yet, about three o'clock in the morning, something happened—my prayer began to change. When I first started to pray, I was concerned only about finding relief. But suddenly it dawned on me that I had offended the Most High God. When I realized that I had a more dreadful problem than missing an ex-girlfriend, I began crying out even more earnestly.

Knowing the gospel of forgiveness, I was compelled to face an angry God. During those moments, it was as if God supernaturally granted me repentance. Sins I had long forgotten were being recalled to my mind. As each one was brought to my attention, I no longer desired to suppress the truth about myself but openly confessed my sins to God. How could I have sinned against such a gracious God?

And after I had finished laying out all my transgressions before the Lord, something happened—the weight of my sin was lifted, and joy filled my soul. I knew I was forgiven. Once we see a merciful God, we do not have to hide and cover up our sins. We do not have to cling to the darkness anymore. The glorious light is no longer frightening but liberating. Moreover, once we embrace the knowledge of Christ, we can embrace the knowledge of God. Not only does Christ *reveal* the Father to us (John 14:9) but He moves our heart to *embrace* the Father.

By observing Christ, we learn about the love and grace of God, and we learn to appreciate the anger and severity of God's justice. By looking at Jesus Christ, we see God's mercy flowing out of God's justice. Because the cross unites God's mercy with God's justice, the truth of God's justice becomes altogether glorious.

This is why the greatest apologetic is the cross. It is the gospel of Jesus Christ that is "the power of God to salvation" (Rom. 1:16). Repentance is a supernatural gift from God (2 Tim. 2:25) because faith is a supernatural "gift of God" (Eph. 2:8). God must give us a new heart with which to see the gospel of forgiveness before we can properly confess, repent, and turn away from our sins. Just as we need light to escape the darkness, we need faith in the gospel to repent from our sins.

The law can expose our sins and inflame our inward sense of guilt, but it is powerless to bring us to deplore our self-righteousness. What moves us away from our self-confidence and our love for the darkness is the knowledge of God's mercy seen in Christ Jesus. True hope, which must be rooted in the truth, is the only thing that can take us out of our slumber.

Jesus is our only hope because He is the only way to the Father: "No one comes to the Father except through Me," He says (John 14:6). If we are going to come to the truth about ourselves and about God, we need Christ. We need to see the glory of God the Father by gazing into the face of Jesus, who died for us (2 Cor. 4:6). We must see Jesus! We must take our eyes off our self-righteousness and look at the righteousness of Christ.

If you are trusting in your good works or in your weak excuses or in a god of your own making to get you to heaven, you are continuing to cling to the darkness. Covering your sins with papier-mâché will only leave you fully exposed on the day of judgment. The light of God's judgment will quickly burn through all your false hope and silly excuses. If you know the truth, it is the darkness that is scary.

There is no need to continue hiding yourself from God when you may be saved by believing in Jesus Christ and turning away from every last drop of self-confidence. Confess your sin and come to the light. Empty yourself and place all your hope in Christ. He is fully sufficient to save you. Do you believe this?

Even for believers the message of forgiveness is an amazing one that we desperately need every day of our lives. We need constant reminding that God is "faithful and just to forgive us our sins and to cleanse us from all unrighteousness" (1 John 1:9). This is why we must live by faith in Jesus Christ.

Without this message, even as Christians we will always run back into the darkness. When we sin, we are tempted to hide ourselves from God. Delaying repentance is our attempt to linger in the shadows. Out of shame, we may not feel like praying. We often think that if we wait, we can clean up a bit and then seek to enter the courts of heaven a little more respectfully. But such thinking is not from God. It is repenting, not waiting, that cleanses the conscience. We need to flee to Christ the moment we fall into sin. If you are struggling in your Christian walk, why do you continue to delay coming back to the light of the gospel? God is willing to forgive you of all your transgressions. With all your heart, confess the truth about your sins and believe the truth about Christ.

Only the truth will set us free from sin (John 8:32). Only the truth will sanctify us (John 17:17). May we never neglect the Scriptures, and may we never take our eyes off Christ. The light of the gospel is not our enemy—it's our only hope.

Conclusion

Do you want the truth? Do you want to know who you are? Do you want to know the depth of your sins? Do you want to know the holiness of God? If so, then run to the light. Flee to Christ. Look into His face—look directly at the One who suffered on the cross. Look intently at the One who suffered in your place. Take a hard look at His compassion, His mercy, His goodness, His humility, and His love for sinners just like you. Look and live, my dear friend. Look at His love until you break. And after you break, keep looking until you are healed.

۞ QUESTIONS FOR REFLECTION

1. Why do we often have a love/hate relationship with the truth?

2. Why is truth so important to us?

3. Why do we want to suppress the truth?

4. How is truth found only in Christ?

$\mathcal{P}$eace

the pursuit of

The world is at war! Since Adam's sin, there has never been any lasting peace on earth. The world has been subjected to violence from the beginning, and it will remain under this dreadful curse until the return of the Prince of Peace, when it "will be delivered from the bondage of corruption" (Rom. 8:21).

It all started when Adam and Eve "shook their fists" at God by defying His authority (Gen. 3:1–6). This act of treason placed them and all of humanity at war with God. Their sin, like every sin, is an attack on God's glory (Rom. 3:23). In justice, God's disposition toward humanity changed from pleasure to anger. In His displeasure, He sent angels with flaming swords to drive out man from His presence.

This cosmic war between God and humanity disrupted the tranquility among all of creation. Adam blamed Eve for his sin, and from that point forward humankind has been hostile toward each other. This was made evident when Cain killed his brother Abel. Since then the whole world has been plummeted into hostilities of every kind.

World wars, civil wars, genocide, terrorism, looting, mothers killing their own babies in the womb, domestic violence, divorce, and siblings fighting over Lego pieces have been the sad effects of humankind's hostility toward God. But this is not all; man is at war with himself. There is no inward peace within the soul of man. As the Lord says through the prophet Isaiah, "There is no peace…for the wicked" (Isa. 48:22). The Bible explains that *external* conflict is derived from *internal* conflict within the heart (James 4:1).

People war with each other because they lack peace within themselves. This internal conflict comes from a defiled conscience toward God and a heart that pants after that which cannot bring satisfaction (James 4:2). Guilt—inward turmoil—comes from a life that is at war with the conscience. More importantly, guilt comes from a life that is at war with God.

Martyn Lloyd-Jones asked, "Why are there wars in the world? Why is there this constant international tension? What is the matter with the world? Why war and all the unhappiness and turmoil and discord amongst men?" Lloyd-Jones went on to answer his own questions: "There is only one answer to these questions—sin. Nothing else; just sin."[1]

Like death, however, war is not natural. God did not design us to be in conflict. In the same way we desire to flee pain, we cannot help but hate war. We long for peace and contentment. Knowingly or unknowingly, we long for a clean conscience before God

Eastern religions view peace, which they call nirvana, as the ultimate goal of salvation. Yet their understanding of peace is an annihilation of the individual consciousness.

---

1. Martyn Lloyd-Jones, *Studies in the Sermon on the Mount* (Grand Rapids: Eerdmans, 1976), 102.

If we ceased to exist, of course we would be free from war. But peace is something more than the absence of conflict. According to the Bible, peace can be experienced only among individuals who are united in one mind and one heart. Perfect peace comes only with perfect love. Peace is best understood by looking at the harmony between the Father, the Son, and the Holy Spirit. And the peace that exists inherently within the Godhead is the peace that we long for in our hearts.

Wrong Ways of Finding Peace
As long as we love ourselves more than we love God, we will look for various ways to eliminate our guilt without having to forsake our sins. Seeking to cover our guilt with *religious activity* is one of the more common methods of suppressing a guilty conscience. Religious activity, however, is nothing more than our attempt to replace our guilt with pride. One way not to feel guilty is by being self-righteous.

Before the apostle Paul's conversion to Christianity, he was a zealous keeper of the law. When it came to external obedience, "the righteousness which is in the law," he believed himself to be "blameless" (Phil. 3:6). He sought to cope with his guilt by boasting in his good works. The more Francis of Assisi became disgusted with his flamboyant lifestyle, the more he deprived himself of pleasure. After Martin Luther vowed to become a monk, he wore himself out trying to gain the favor of God with prayers and confession. Likewise, we are tempted to take pride in our religious activities. Seeking to eliminate our guilt with religious activity, however, is tiring—not to mention impossible. "By the works of the law no flesh shall be justified," writes Paul (Gal. 2:16). A lifetime of good cannot cancel out a single black stain. Though we may attempt to compensate for our guilt, we remain condemned by our conscience before God.

If we have become disillusioned with religious activity, we may be tempted to cope with our guilt *by lowering the standard*. To get our conscience to go easy on us, we often fill our thoughts with moral excuses like these: I could not help it. It wasn't my fault. I tried to do what was right. I have made a few mistakes, but at least I am not as bad as most of my friends.

Two things are required to cope with guilt in this fashion. First, we have to lower God's standard for right and wrong. Because perfection is an impossible mark to meet, we must create a more reachable standard. Second, we have to raise our opinion of ourselves. In other words, we must have a low view of God and a high view of ourselves. Or, as the Bible says, we must suppress the truth about God by creating a god in our own image, "made like corruptible man" (Rom. 1:23).

Some people have given moral excuses by going as far as to use their God-given intelligence to deny the existence of God. If we can convince ourselves that there is no God, then we can seek to ease our conscience by saying there is no objective standard of morality. With no divine lawgiver, we can tell our conscience that morality is only a social construct. And once the standard of morality is placed on a sliding scale, we can adjust the standard in accord with our own behavior.

Yet finding peace by lowering the standard does not help us cope, and it also ends in failure. Though we may say that morals are only relative and there are no absolutes, our conscience continues to condemn us. We may craft a web of excuses, but we will remain internally frustrated with ourselves. This is because we know—deep down—that a holy God will judge us for our sins. Though we may try, we cannot entirely suppress the knowledge of a righteous God.

Another way of muting our consciences is by keeping our minds so busy that we do not have time to think about eternal realities. It is not uncommon for people to cope with their guilt by *distracting themselves* with hedonistic pleasures. A counselee who was involved in sexual immorality once told me that the only way he was able to overcome his shame was by diverting his thoughts. Alcohol and drugs often provide people with such a diversion. Movies offer an escape by pulling our thoughts and emotions into an alternate reality. Night clubs, sporting events, and Hollywood are big business because of the ever-increasing demand for entertainment. The world is running to and fro from one distraction to the next—and much of this distraction is designed to keep people's minds from falling into despair.

Distraction, however, does not mute the guilty conscience. This method works only if we never rest. Some people attempt to stay intoxicated, but sooner or later we are all going to have to face reality. We may want to push our problems off until tomorrow, but deep down we know that the day is coming when we will no longer be able to hide from God.

Regardless of how we may try to conceal our shame and find peace, our shame and inward turmoil refuse to be silenced because "he who covers his sins will not prosper" (Prov. 28:13). Once we are judged guilty by the law that God has written on our conscience, the stain is too deep for us to cleanse. A guilty conscience will continue to wage war within all of us who are condemned by God. "'There is no peace,' says the LORD, 'for the wicked'" (Isa. 48:22).

The Only Way to Find Peace

How can the guilty obtain a clean conscience? How can sinners find peace with God? How can we be made right before God? Is peace with God even possible? This is the most important question in life.

Though we have sinned against a just God, He offers us forgiveness in His Son. The Son of God did not come in His first appearing as a mighty warrior seeking to take vengeance. Rather, Christ came in love, with the holy angels declaring, "Glory to God in the highest, and on earth peace, goodwill toward men!" (Luke 2:14). He came not to judge but to mercifully offer us the terms of peace.

Though Christ demands full surrender on our part, He is the one who did all the work to bring peace between us and God. As a man, Christ earned perfect and complete righteousness by His sinless obedience. As evidence of His sinlessness, Christ rose from the dead (Acts 2:24), and it is this righteousness that He offers to transfer to our account. Moreover, He offers to transfer our sins to His account, as He paid the penalty for sins when He bore the full wrath of God on the cross (Isa. 53:4–5). Christ has done all the work to redeem and reconcile us to God. He extends forgiveness to us by offering us His righteousness for free. And His forgiveness and righteousness are the two things we need to be justified, or declared right, by God.

But the question remains, What does the Holy Spirit work within us when we are justified by God? According to

Christ, two things transpire when we obtain peace with God. First, by the Spirit's grace, we must acknowledge that we have no righteousness of our own. We must confess that we are sinners who deserve eternal punishment. More than that, we must desire to be forgiven of our sins. We must repent and follow the example of the psalmist, who said,

> I acknowledged my sin to You,
> And my iniquity I have not hidden.
> I said, "I will confess my transgressions to the LORD,"
> And You forgave the iniquity of my sin. (Ps. 32:5)

Jerry Bridges reminds us that "our heart is deceitful. It excuses, rationalizes, and justifies our actions. It blinds us to entire areas of sin in our lives."[2] Therefore, we need to follow David's example, who cried out to God:

> Search me, O God, and know my heart;
> Try me, and know my anxieties;
> And see if there is any wicked way in me,
> And lead me in the way everlasting. (Ps. 139:23–24)

And again He prayed:

> Have mercy upon me, O God,
> According to Your lovingkindness;
> According to the multitude of Your tender mercies,
> Blot out my transgressions.
> Wash me thoroughly from my iniquity,
> And cleanse me from my sin.

---

2. Jerry Bridges, *The Pursuit of Holiness* (Colorado Springs, Colo.: Nav-Press, 2006), 61.

For I acknowledge my transgressions,
And my sin is always before me. (Ps. 51:1–3)

But repentance is not all that is required of us; we must believe the gospel. We must have faith in Christ as the only means of forgiveness and righteousness. Our repentance and faith do not earn peace with God but rather the opposite— they show we are fully dependent on the righteousness of Christ for our salvation.

According to the Scriptures, faith alone justifies us because faith unites us to the righteousness of Christ. As the Puritan William Gurnall remarked: "We are justified, not by giving anything to God—what we do—but by receiving from God, what Christ hath done for us."[3] Only by resting in the finished work of Christ, by the grace of the Holy Spirit, will we ever have peace with God: "Therefore, having been justified by faith, we have peace with God through our Lord Jesus Christ" (Rom. 5:1).

Martin Luther experienced this peace only after he stopped trying to earn his way to God through personal piety and good works. He claimed, "Night and day I pondered until I saw the connection between the justice of God and the statement that 'the just shall live by his faith.' Then I grasped that the justice of God is that righteousness by which through grace and sheer mercy God justifies us through faith. Thereupon I felt myself to be reborn and to have gone through open doors into paradise."[4]

---

3. Gurnall, *Christian in Complete Armour*, 433.
4. As quoted in Roland H. Bainton, *Here I Stand: A Life of Martin Luther* (Peabody, Mass.: Hendrickson, 2009), 48.

Conclusion

Without peace with God there is no peace with self. No matter how defiled we are, our sins can be forgiven through the blood of Jesus Christ. We must stop making excuses for our sins, stop trying to earn God's forgiveness by attempting to do good works, and stop trying to suppress the knowledge of our guilt. A clean conscience before God is found only in Christ Jesus. We need to repent of our sins and believe the message of the gospel with all our mind, our heart, and our strength. If you have no peace, then cast yourself completely on God's mercy, which is promised in Christ Jesus. If you believe this, you will be forgiven. This is the promise of God.

⚜ QUESTIONS FOR REFLECTION

1. Why do we crave and need peace?

2. What is the cause of conflict?

3. What are some wrong ways we try to clean our consciences?

4. Why is Christ the Prince of Peace?

5. How is peace found only in Christ?

8

Holiness the pursuit of

Everyone wants to be good—at least everyone starts out wanting to be good. Some people become so hardened in their sins that they no longer care about doing what's right, but this attitude was not always the case. It is not normal for children to want to grow up to be the next Adolf Hitler. Hardened criminals did not sear their consciences overnight. It typically takes time for depraved souls to consciously aspire to be evil.

I remember when I was a teenager and I sneaked out of my parents' house for the first time to smoke a cigarette. I had resisted the temptation for weeks, but somehow I talked myself into trying it. Afterward I remember feeling guilty—I knew my parents would be disappointed in me if they ever learned what had happened. At that point, I did not want to smoke again. But I guess I thought smoking was cool because it was not long before I was able to smoke with my friends on a regular basis. And this is the nature of almost every sin—the more we give in to temptation, the easier it becomes to override our conscience.

Though people may admit that they have picked up a few bad habits over the years, few will admit to being a bad person. Gangsters still have a sense of morality among themselves. The great majority of those locked away in prison view themselves as being relatively good people. Moreover, humankind is religious by nature. Shrines, temples, mosques, and churches cover the globe. Almost everyone prays every now and then. Even those who have rejected religion often aspire to be decent citizens. Atheists do not typically think it is good to be cruel to others.

The Wrong Way to Pursue Holiness

We may think non-Christians do not want to be good, but this is a misunderstanding of the doctrine of depravity. Though humankind is not good, they have not given up their desire to be good—at least good in a relative sense. We must remember that the religions of the world are all based on obtaining eternal life and peace through good works.

Yet this is another reason for people's frustration. Though people have a conscience that preaches purity to them, they know they're already defiled by sin. Though they would love to avoid the feeling of shame, they enjoy daydreaming about shameful things. Depraved humans are frustrated because they are equipped with a conscience, for the same conscience that pushes them to do good is the conscience that continuously condemns them for doing bad. This frustration causes them to be conflicted. They love to sin, but they still aspire to be good. Somehow, they need to find a way to enjoy their sin while hanging on to the notion that they are not bad people.

Some people seek to hide their moral failure and self-centeredness by *trying hard to do good*. "As long as my good deeds outweigh my mistakes, all is well," they think to themselves. Each failure must be compensated with acts of generosity. Though they may admit that they are not perfect, they take comfort in all the good things they have done. By going to church, giving to the poor, donating clothes to the local shelter, and other such deeds they can feel good about themselves. "Mortification from a self-strength," according to John Owen, "carried on by ways of self-invention, unto the end of a self-righteousness is the soul and substance of all false religion."[1]

The problem is that people's desire to be good is not as strong as their desire to please themselves. Unbelievers are in bondage to their sinful nature, and their sinful nature always taints even their best attempts to do what is right. They may think they are doing good. They may even think they are pleasing God with all their religious acts of worship. They may give money to the poor, plant a tree in the forest, say long prayers, go to confession, and refrain from many evil devices, but all the while (due to the motives of their hearts), they are never able to do a single good deed. Even their desire to do good is tainted by sin. The problem lies in their motives. For any act to be good, it must arise out of a desire to please God. To do something good, God's glory must be the principal motive. But because the heart of an unbeliever remains in opposition to God, the unbeliever "cannot please God" (Rom. 8:8).

Unbelievers may have a desire to be good, but they do not—and cannot—desire to place God's glory above themselves. They may be moved to escape the wrath of God or to

---

1. John Owen, *The Mortification of Sin*, in *The Works of John Owen*, ed. William H. Goold (Edinburgh: Banner of Truth, 2009), 6:7.

gain some eternal treasure, but it is impossible for them to love God more than they love themselves. They may desire to serve God for the advantages, but they cannot submit their lives to God out of the mere joy of it. They may give to the poor, but their motives for doing so will be self-serving. Some pray to be seen by others. Some give to charity to ease their conscience. Like the philanthropists who enjoy positive publicity when they make large donations to charity, sinners are motivated to do what is right only out of selfish reasons. Thus, their desire for goodness is only a relative goodness that comes "short of the glory of God" (Rom. 3:23).

Humanists and environmentalists, those who desire to help humankind, fall short of being good as well. In their attempts to be good people, they have exalted people and creation over the Creator. They have made an idol out of the world. They have placed the good of human beings above the glory of God.

Yet the first commandment has to be fulfilled before any of the other commandments can be rightly followed. That is, we must love God with all our heart, soul, and strength before our motives are pleasing to God (Deut. 6:5). Anything less than this is sin. God says that the value of all our righteousness is equivalent to "filthy rags" (Isa. 64:6). When reflecting on his life as a passionate Pharisee, possessing a zeal that surpassed all his peers, Paul considered his best efforts to have a negative value (Phil. 3:7). Even if we could eliminate our sin and place only our good deeds on the scale of God's justice, we would still come up short. The best we have to offer is considered as "rubbish" in the sight of God (Phil. 3:8). This is because our best is tainted with sinful motives.

Not only is there "none who does good" (Rom. 3:12), there is none who can do good (Rom. 8:8). All humanity is conceived in sin and "brought forth in iniquity" (Ps. 51:5). An infant comes forth from its mother's womb "speaking lies" (Ps. 58:3). Children do not have to be taught to be selfish; it comes naturally to them because we are born enslaved to sin (Eph. 2:1).

Sin has not simply touched us from without; it has deeply penetrated our hearts. It flows out of our nature. We are not just depraved—we are *totally* depraved. There is no part of us that sin has not penetrated and defiled. Our thoughts, affections, and deeds are thoroughly tainted by sin. As Louis Berkhof explained: "Sin does not reside in any one faculty of the soul, but in the heart, which in Scriptural psychology is the central organ of the soul, out of which are the issues of life. And from this center its influence and operations spread to the intellect, the will, the affections, in short, to the entire man, including his body."[2]

So our pursuit of holiness in our own strength always ends in frustration, and deep down we know it. Regardless of the many ways we may seek to eliminate our guilt, all our effort ends in frustration. This frustration, moreover, is the result of wanting to be good without wanting to humbly submit to God.

Self-reliance, or confidence in the flesh, always leads us into greater bondage (Rom. 7:5). The good we may want to do, even as believers, we will find ourselves unable to carry out in our own power (Rom. 7:19). Though we may give our

---

2. Louis Berkhof, *Systematic Theology* (Grand Rapids: Eerdmans, 1994), 233.

best effort at keeping God's law, the law of sin that is at work in our lives will always cause us to be frustrated (Rom. 7:23).

A self-focused and self-reliant obedience will always lead to either pride or despair. Either we will look down on those who do not do as we do, or we will become discouraged because we are unable, in our own strength, to obey God. Because a self-reliant obedience is a self-centered obedience, it will not please God. If we are motivated by the sin of self-ishness, how can we expect to obey God?

The Right Way to Pursue Holiness

The Bible makes it clear that "those who are in the flesh cannot please God" (Rom. 8:8). No matter how hard we may try to obey God in our own might, we will be unable to rise above our own selfish motives.

Be Filled with the Holy Spirit

The prerequisite to living a holy life is dying to our flesh and being made alive to Christ by the Holy Spirit (Rom. 8:2). We have to die to the proud notion that we are able, in the power and resolve of our own flesh, to keep the law. We need a new nature that is filled with the love of God. We must be "born again" by the power of the Spirit (John 3:7). We need our old nature to be "crucified with Christ" (Gal. 2:20) and the "love of God…poured out in our hearts" (Rom. 5:5), and this requires supernatural assistance. Only when God's love is operating within us can we love God and our neighbors properly. Only with a new nature that is empowered by the Holy Spirit can we produce the fruit of the Spirit and have the pure motives needed to please God.

Sanctification is the process by which believers are made holy. It is neither the work of God alone, where we passively "let go and let God," nor is it the work of man alone, where we "pull ourselves up by our own bootstraps." Rather, as Jerry Bridges explains, "Sanctification is not a partnership with the Spirit in the sense that we each—the believer and the Holy Spirit—do our respective tasks. Rather, we work as He enables us to work. His work lies behind all our work and makes our work possible."[3] That is, though we work, it is God who empowers the work within us (Phil. 2:13).

Thus, holiness comes only from God working in us. We must be empowered from above to unselfishly love God. And it is only when we love God that "His commandments are not burdensome" (1 John 5:3). In short, to love God we must be filled and controlled by the Holy Spirit.

Faith

Yet how are we to be filled with the Spirit? Though being filled with the Spirit sounds difficult and mysterious, it is something promised to all who believe. The key to being controlled by the Spirit is to have faith in God. We must believe.

We are not only justified by faith; we are also sanctified by faith. The reason faith is vital is because faith unites us to the power of God. "Without Me," the Lord said, "you can do nothing" (John 15:5). It is only if we abide in Him, as He is the vine, that we will be able to bear fruit (John 15:4). Likewise, the fruit of the Spirit (Gal. 5:22–23) only comes as

---

3. Jerry Bridges, *Holiness Day by Day* (Colorado Springs, Colo.: NavPress, 2008), 221.

we are filled with the Spirit. Thus, we can be fruitful in our Christian lives only as we are united to God by faith.

Faith unites us to Christ because it is not self-focused or self-reliant. Rather, faith is dependent on God as it looks to Him for the power and the strength to obey Him. "Without faith," the Bible says, "it is impossible to please [God]" (Heb. 11:6). Though we cannot please God in our own power, we are not deserted to battle sin in our own power. Victory over sin is promised to all of us who believe. But this is the essence of faith—not trusting in self but relying on God. Not only does faith include standing on the reality that our old, self-ish nature has been defeated and crucified in Christ but it enables us to walk in a manner pleasing to God. We can do nothing greater than to believe the promises of God.

Faith not only believes that God exists but it believes that God is "a rewarder of those who diligently seek Him" (Heb. 11:6). It is by faith that we turn our backs on this world and willingly endure the sufferings and reproaches of Christ (Heb. 11:26). By faith we see that the things that are invisible are more eternal and beneficial than the things that can be seen (2 Cor. 4:18).

By faith we are united to the love of God in Christ Jesus (Eph. 3:17–19), and only by love, which comes by faith in Christ, can we please God. And this is why faith "is the victory that has overcome the world" (1 John 5:4).

Repentance
By faith we renounce this world and run to Christ. This is why God-given *repentance* is also necessary to live a holy life, for it could be said that change begins with repentance.

Repentance includes not only turning away from a life of sin but also turning away from all self-confidence and self-righteousness (Phil. 3:4–7). It includes humbling ourselves before God and confessing that we can do nothing pleasing in His sight (Rom. 8:8). It is admitting that without divine grace, we are incapable of obeying God.

For Christians, repentance, like faith, is not a one-time event. "Repentance is not merely the start of the Christian life," according to John Calvin; "it is the Christian life."[4] If we are going to overcome sin, we must begin with acknowledging our failures before God. If we think "we have no sin, we deceive ourselves" (1 John 1:8). Pride, as do all forms of conceit, leads us away from trusting Christ.

Yet victory over sin begins with acknowledging and confessing our sins before God. If we are struggling with pride, anger, lust, or any other besetting sin, we must first clear our conscience before God and humbly look to Christ for help. Humbling ourselves before God is always the first step.

Repentance, moreover, includes four things. First, repentance is *confessing* our sins before God. Change always begins here. We are not going to overcome any shortcoming until we acknowledge the shortcoming as sin before the Lord. Confession is identifying our sin for what it is—transgression against God. Identifying sin as sin is a must. It is easier to identify our sin as a mistake or a weakness because it is difficult to confess that we have knowingly transgressed against a holy and just God.

---

4. As quoted in Joel Beeke, "Calvin on Piety," in *The Cambridge Companion to John Calvin*, ed. Donald K. McKim (Cambridge: Cambridge University Press, 2004), 141.

Moreover, it is easier to give in to temptation when we fail to draw the line between right and wrong. It is not until we are convinced that our thoughts, emotions, and actions are sin that we will begin to be motivated to repent and to resist such temptation in the future.

But this first step is more than calling sin what it is; it is admitting that we have willfully committed it. This is impossible for prideful and self-righteous people to do. The drunkard is more likely to admit that he enjoys drinking than he is to openly confess that he is an alcoholic. There is no change, however, when we refuse to confess our transgressions (Prov. 28:13). Thus, confession of sin is the first step in repentance.

Second, repentance is *taking responsibility* for our sins. Repentance is more than confession. It also includes taking ownership of our sins. Alcoholics may admit they are addicted to alcohol, but this alone does not indicate that they believe they are at fault. Maybe they think it is their problems that have driven them to drink.

But, according to the Bible, no matter the unusual circumstances, there is no justification for sin. We cannot say, "I could not help it," or "It was not my fault." Any excuse is a failure to accept the blame. Adam blamed Eve, Eve blamed the serpent, and we often blame our spouse or our children or our circumstances. But shifting the blame is not true repentance.

Marriage problems, for instance, will never be fully resolved as long as a husband and wife continue to blame each other for their own sinful behavior. It is easier to be angry with your spouse when he or she is mistreating you, but this is not an excuse for your sins. We are called to be holy in an unholy world while surrounded by unholy people.

Being holy is never dependent on the behavior of others. We are called to love others even when they intentionally mistreat us (Prov. 19:11). Our love for our spouses is not contingent on their love for us. We are to do them good, walk the extra mile, turn the other cheek, and pray for them, even when they are purposefully exploiting us (Matt. 5:43–44). So what must we do to live a pure life? We are to stop making excuses and take ownership of our sins before God and before all those we have knowingly sinned against.

Third, repentance is *expressing heartfelt remorse* for our sins. Without sorrow, repentance means nothing. Some people may acknowledge their sin and even admit that they are guilty, but these first two steps alone are not full repentance. Some people do not care that they are guilty. Many drivers who are ticketed for speeding may wish they had not gotten caught, but few actually feel guilty that they were driving too fast. And this is why we must distinguish between the feeling of regret for getting caught and the feeling of regret for actually doing something wrong. The difference between the two kinds of regretful feelings is the same difference we see between love and selfishness.

For instance, I remember skipping school without my parents' knowledge and going to the lake with my friends. All was going well until I was pulled over for speeding. Driving home, I knew I would not be able to avoid the displeasure of my parents and the consequences that would follow. The best way to minimize my trouble, I thought to myself, was to confess everything to my parents as soon as I saw them.

And this seemed to work. My parents were so impressed with my confession that they paid my speeding ticket. Yet my repentance was not true repentance. I was not remorseful for speeding or for skipping school. I was merely upset that I got caught. My repentance, though emotionally felt, was motivated by my selfish desire to avoid the consequences of my actions.

Real remorse, on the other hand, is not motivated by self-interest but stems from a concern for others. It feels bad for the hurt and pain that was wrongly inflicted on the ones we injured. The repentant and remorseful heart cannot help but want to make things right, even if this means embracing the consequences.

Fourth, repentance is *turning away* from our sins (Acts 3:19). The heart of repentance is change. We are not sorry for our sins if we are not willing to forsake our sins. As long as we love our transgressions, we are not sorry for them. This is why salvation is only for those who are awakened to their great need and who want to be delivered from their sins.

Because Christians can never boast of being free from sin, repentance and the war against sin must be continuous. In other words, turning from sin is not a one-time event. Though as believers we have been delivered from the bondage of sin, we are not free to retreat from our battle against indwelling sin.

Mortification

Consequently, if we want to live holy lives, we must not only repent of our sins but we must *mortify*—"put to death"—the lusts of our flesh (Rom. 8:13). To mortify our sinful desires means to unmercifully slaughter every sinful thought before it unmercifully slaughters us. As John Owen warned, "Be killing sin or it will be killing you."[5] Practically speaking, mortification consists of resisting temptation by cutting off temptation. If our hand leads us astray, then we should cut it off; if our eye offends us, according to Christ, then we are to pluck it out (Matt. 18:8–9). If it is better to go to heaven lame than to go to hell able-bodied, then how much more should we be willing to do away with such things as the internet or smartphones if they are constantly leading us into sin?

Whatever hinders our walk with Christ needs to be eliminated from our lives (Heb. 12:1). It is said that the wise man avoids walking by the harlot's house (Prov. 5:8), and if we would follow the wise man's example, we would do well to travel the extra mile to avoid unnecessary temptation.

The victory over temptation is not won simply by excommunicating certain sinful activities from our lives. It includes replacing those sinful activities with spiritual disciplines. Rather than gazing at various images on our phones, we should gaze our mind's eye on Christ. We can replace the temptation that comes from watching television with reading and memorizing the Scriptures. Rather than doing activities that we know often lead to temptation, we can use that time to pray and seek the Lord. We must replace every sin that we leave behind with an activity that drives our minds and hearts to God.

Spiritual Disciplines

If it is by faith that we are empowered by the Spirit to repent and mortify our fleshly desires, then how are we to grow

---

5. Owen, *Mortification of Sin*, in *Works*, 6:9.

in faith? The Bible gives us the answer when it says, "Faith comes by hearing, and hearing by the word of God" (Rom. 10:17). This is important because we learn that the key to holiness is faith, and the key to faith is God's Word. We must grow in grace and in knowledge. We are charged not to "be conformed to this world, but [to] be transformed by the renewing of [our] mind[s]" (Rom. 12:2).

God has chosen to sanctify us by the power of the Spirit through "belief in the truth" (2 Thess. 2:13). And this is why Jesus prayed that we would be sanctified by the truth (John 17:17). This means that we must continuously refocus our minds and our hearts on heavenly things (Col. 3:1–2).

When we gaze on Christ by faith, we are changed into His likeness (2 Cor. 3:18). When we see His glory, we cannot help but love Him. And as Henry Scougal reminds us, "We become what we love."[6] With great admiration, we will seek to emulate His humility, patience, and love. Moreover, once our minds see the glory and excellence of Christ, the things of this world—that foolishly captivate and seduce the world—will begin to loosen their grip on our lives. We will come to despise the dirty rags of this world when we behold the holy garments of the One who died for us.

Too often, however, we find ourselves operating in the flesh because we have unwittingly grown cold toward the things of God. Our hearts are easily preoccupied by the cares and concerns of this world. Fervency for God can quickly cool when we take our minds off Christ. And when our minds are not fixed on Christ, it is easy for our faith to fail and for us to be controlled by the flesh.

---

6. Scougal, *Life of God in the Soul of Man*, 46.

Bible Intake

Therefore, reading the Bible, listening to sermons, and meditating on the promises of God are vital parts of growing in grace and in the knowledge of the Lord. If our minds are not consistently pulled upward, then they will be irresistibly dragged downward by the perpetual distractions of this world. Yet the remedy to a carnal mind is simple—consistent intake of the Word of God.

By hiding the Word of God in our hearts, we will be able to overcome sin (Ps. 119:11). By meditating on the Scriptures and rehearsing spiritual songs in our hearts, we will gradually be less and less gripped by the things of this world. By memorizing Scripture verses, we will be able to cling to the promises of God when trials and temptations come. In short, the Bible must be constantly going into us if we want the love of Christ to be constantly flowing out of us.

Prayer

Moreover, when temptation does come, we must quickly cry out to God for help, for prayer is the evidence that we are not relying on ourselves. God knows what we need even before we ask, but the reason we do not receive from God is because we fail to plead with God (James 4:3). Too much self-confidence keeps us from fervently begging God to come to our aid. Yet because there never is a time we do not fervently need God, there is never a time we do not need to pray to God. Praying without ceasing is the evidence of abiding in Christ (1 Thess. 5:17).

Conclusion

Though we may be born with a desire to be good, we remain unable to please God. Our problem lies in our motive. Because it is impossible without the grace of God to love God above ourselves, even our best efforts come short of the glory of God. Enslaved to sin we remain until we repent of our sins and look to Christ in faith. By faith in God we are not only born again but are empowered by the Spirit to live acceptable lives before God. The key to holiness is walking in the Spirit by faith through the continual renewal of our minds with prayer and Bible intake.

❧ QUESTIONS FOR REFLECTION

1. Why is goodness a universal pursuit?

2. Why is it that sin is a universal problem?

3. Why are the motives of our heart so important?

4. For believers, what are some of the key spiritual issues that lead to holiness?

5. How is holiness found only in Christ?

the pursuit of
Life

We were born to live! That is to say, the instinct for life is in us all. But the life we long for is greater than mere existence. We naturally long for something more than being artificially kept alive. Who aspires to live forever in a coma? Who wants to be stuck in a hospital bed indefinitely? Who wishes for irreversible brain damage? Yes, we want to live life, but the life we want to live is a life of glory, happiness, purpose, freedom, companionship, truth, peace, and holiness.

The life we aspire after is greater than the definition of *life* provided to us by biologists, who tend to flatten out the meaning of life. Some define it by observing the differences of animals and plants from inorganic matter, such as the capacity for growth, reproduction, functional activity, and change. Others define *life* as "the quality that distinguishes a vital and functional being from a dead body."[1]

Yet the *life* that God speaks about consists of something more than the qualities that exist in unconscious plant life or within conscious animals. Life, according to the Bible, can be

---

1. Merriam-Webster Online, s.v. "life," accessed April 26, 2017, https://www.merriamwebster.com/dictionary.

understood only by understanding the author, giver, and sustainer of life, God. This is because, in the truest sense, God is "life" (John 1:4; Acts 17:25).

Thus, according to the Scriptures, life comes only through *union with God*. More precisely, life is found only in an unbroken covenantal relationship with God. Animals and vegetation have a form of life as they live, move, and have their being in God, but only man was created to enjoy a covenantal relationship with the author of life Himself.

In the beginning, man became a living soul when God breathed out of Himself the breath of life into him (Gen. 2:7). The glory, happiness, purpose, freedom, companionship, truth, peace, and holiness that come through covenant life with God would only continue, however, if man remained upright. Only if man obeyed the condition of the covenant, which was clearly manifested in the command not to eat of the fruit of the tree of the knowledge of good and evil (Gen. 2:17), would he then live before God.

Death entered because man's covenant relationship with God was broken. Death, therefore, is to be understood as *separation* from God. In other words, death is not the absence of existence but the absence of a personal relationship with God.

Man was made to enjoy God and participate in the mutual love between the Father, Son, and Holy Spirit. Personal happiness is found only by participating within this glorious relationship. Being cut off and separated from the life of God is the consequence and penalty of sin. Misery, meaninglessness, bondage, guilt, unrighteousness, and shame are the result of this broken and adverse relationship.

Moreover, death and separation from God take place in three stages. All three stages, however, were initiated the day that Adam sinned (Gen. 2:17). The first stage is *spiritual death*, which is when man became hostile toward God. The second stage is *physical death*, which is when man is cut off from any hope of reconciliation with God. The third stage is *eternal death*, which is when man is cast into the fire of God's wrath, away from the presence of God where all traces of happiness, meaning, freedom, truth, and glory are forever removed. Each of these stages is a further removal of the life of God from the soul of man.

Though sin has turned our hearts away from God, sin has not canceled our innate longing for the happiness, purpose, freedom, companionship, truth, peace, holiness, and glory that comes only from a relationship with God. Though we may desire heaven without God, without God there is no heaven. In sum, to find glory, happiness, purpose, freedom, companionship, truth, peace, and holiness, we must find life. To find life, however, we must find God.

Christ Is Our Life
Finding life means that we need reconciliation with God. But the only way to be reconciled to God is through faith in Christ Jesus. Christ says, "I am the way, the truth, and the life. No one comes to the Father except through Me" (John 14:6). As Christ says elsewhere, "He who believes in the Son has everlasting life; and he who does not believe the Son shall not see life, but the wrath of God abides on him" (John 3:36).

This is why it is crucial for us to have a personal relationship with Jesus Christ to have life and a relationship with

God: "And this is eternal life, that they may know You, the only true God, and Jesus Christ whom You have sent" (John 17:3). As the Bible says in another place: "God has given us eternal life, and this life is in His Son. He who has the Son has life; he who does not have the Son of God does not have life" (1 John 5:11–12).

Moreover, it is an abundant life that Christ gives (John 10:10). By bringing us into a loving relationship with the Father, we not only receive eternal life, we receive a life of joy, peace, and purpose. It is an abundant life because it is the life of Christ that is lived within us who believe (Gal. 2:20). And the life of Christ within us is like an everlasting river that quenches all our thirsts (John 4:14).

Christ Is Our Joy

By receiving the life of Christ, we receive the joy of Christ. That is, the joy of the Lord becomes our joy (John 15:11). What kind of joy is this? It is a "joy inexpressible and full of glory" (1 Peter 1:8). It is a joy that made Christ the happiest person who has ever lived (Heb. 1:9).

In fact, Christ never lost His joy. Though He was "a Man of sorrows" (Isa. 53:3), He was able to rejoice in the midst of His suffering. Though Christ was called to face and carry out some difficult things, He always found pleasure in obeying God in those things (John 4:34). Even the most difficult task of all—dying on the cross—was motivated by "the joy that was set before Him" (Heb. 12:2). He was full of joy because He delighted in His Father at all times. Christ understood that in the presence of God there "is fullness of joy" (Ps. 16:11). With His heart steadfastly fixed on God, He was anointed with the oil of joy above anyone else (Ps. 45:7). Oh, what a blessing to be able to rejoice in every situation (Phil. 4:4; 1 Thess. 5:16)!

Yet what causes us to cease from rejoicing is not trials and tribulations, but sin. Sin, by its very nature, makes us miserable. It makes us distrust God. It makes us thirsty and brings discontentment into our souls because it separates us from God. Though sin continues to promise us happiness, it only intensifies our dissatisfaction with life. The problem with sin is that it not only enlarges the insatiable appetites of our flesh but it pulls our hearts away from the Lord, the only real source of life and happiness. Thus, sin always leads to misery and death.

What must we do to enter into the joy of the Lord? We must run back into the presence of Christ. We must turn our eyes away from the things of this world and gaze on the altogether lovely One. Only when we are satisfied with Christ will we be satisfied at all.

Christ Is Our All

Christ brings us not only satisfaction but glory, happiness, purpose, freedom, companionship, truth, peace, and holiness because He brings us to the source of all these things—God. We are complete in Christ (Col. 2:10).

Because of Christ, we not only live but we have reason to live (Phil. 1:21). In Christ we have been set free from the bondage of sin. With Christ we have been given true companionship, "a friend who sticks closer than a brother" (Prov. 18:24). We have been given a friend who not only laid down His life for us but who has risen to the highest seat of power to personally intercede for us before God.

Truth, peace, and holiness have been delivered to us in Christ Jesus. He is God. He is our Savior. He is our Lord. He is our hope. He is our righteousness. He is our peace. He is our glory. He is the center of the universe and the center of our lives. He is our life. He is our all in all.

Conclusion

We are searching for something. We cannot help but search for it. We cannot stop searching even if we tried. God has made us to need certain things, such as purpose, happiness, and freedom. Yet because we are born without these things, we are born in pursuit of them. But we are also born blind—blinded by sin and by the passions of our flesh. Because we are born blinded to the beauty and glory of the invisible Christ, our hearts from birth are fixed on the sensorial and temporal passions of this world. We are born deceived, thinking that if we feed our bodily appetites, we will be able to fulfill the deep longings of our hearts. But the deep longings of our hearts continue to remain unsatisfied as our bodily appetites only become more and more insatiable.

We cannot help but know that the world with its passions is passing away (1 John 2:17). Yes, we need eternal glory, happiness, purpose, freedom, companionship, truth, peace, holiness, and life, but these deep-seated longings are fulfilled only in knowing the Lord of glory. In the end, the *unadulterated glory* that we are searching for is the Lord Jesus Christ.

ৡ QUESTIONS FOR REFLECTION

1. What is the meaning of life?

2. Why is life connected to a relationship with God?

3. Why does sin lead to death?

4. Why is life found only in Christ?